Letters to New Disciples

THOMAS A. JONES

Letters to New Disciples

Practical advice
for those
who have decided
to follow Jesus

DPI
DISCIPLESHIP
PUBLICATIONS
INTERNATIONAL

Letters to New Disciples
©1997 by Discipleship Publications International
2 Sterling Road, Billerica MA 01862-2595

Printed in the United States of America

Book design: Chris Costello
Images ©1997 PhotoDisc, Inc.

ISBN 1-57782-048-7

To Amy, Bethany and Corrie.
You have blessed your mother and me
first as children, then as young disciples
and now as treasured friends.

Contents

Acknowledgments

No book ever gets into print without the help of many people. One or two people usually have their names on the cover, but a host of others contribute in important ways. I want to first thank my wife, Sheila, who is this editor's best editor. Her valuable suggestions improved every chapter, and her partnership in every area of life improves everything about me. I also want to thank our three children. This book is dedicated to them because they are more than all I could have asked or imagined.

I want to thank Lisa Morris, our editorial assistant at DPI, and Kim Hanson, our assistant editor, for their helpful ideas and insightful questions. Kim has made significant contributions to almost every book that DPI has published, and she makes equally significant contributions to the spirit of the DPI team every day.

I also want to thank Chris Costello and his assistant, Chad Crossland, for their excellent work in graphics and design. Chris is a world-class designer and our book covers are second to none because of his talent, skill and humility. Chad is a great disciple who has just recently joined our team, but already he is a valuable member.

My thanks also to Larry Wood, Gordon Ferguson, Randy McKean and Dan Bathon. Larry, as our managing editor, has lightened my load tremendously, making it possible for me to have more time to write. Gordon is a trusted friend, fellow writer, and mentor who provides wise counsel. Randy and Dan originally envisioned the publishing ministry that God has blessed for the last five years, and they have given us much-needed encouragement, direction and challenge.

Most of all I give thanks to God who has allowed us to be partners with him in sharing his Good News with people around the world.

Preface
Why These Letters?

About a year ago I wrote some things down to share with a group of new Christians. I had been asked to speak to them about their new lives in Christ, and I wanted to have something to give them to read and reflect on later. Several months afterward I was talking with a disciple who had just recently made his decision to follow Jesus. He told me that someone had given him the material I had written for the group, and he had found it so helpful that he had read it every day for three weeks. My talk with him convinced me that something more was needed along these lines, and thus was born the idea for this book.

Those of you who read this will have your own unique set of backgrounds, circumstances, personalities and needs. I am not pretending here that I can say everything you need to hear. You have people in your lives who know you well and who walk with God daily. They are your best sources for guidance and advice. But I do believe many of us are helped by having concise written statements of God's plan for our lives that we can read and reread.

I am a writer, but, as you might suspect, I am also a reader. More than that, I am a "rereader"—that is, one who reads some of the same things over and over. When I first made a commitment to follow Jesus Christ, I was introduced to a little book that helped me understand the reasonableness of my faith. Because I was a natural doubter, I found it most helpful to read this little book several times. Its message eventually took root deep in my thinking. My goal with these letters is to give you something you will not just read once, but something you can read again and again until its message gets deep inside you.

More than twenty years ago, I put together some material for new Christians that we called *Your First Forty Days*. Later it was expanded and published under a different title. Still later, it was revised and is in print today under the title *Deep Convictions*. Chances are that the person who gave you this book of letters also gave you a copy of *Deep Convictions*. Let me say clearly that this book you are reading now was not designed to replace the material you will find in *Deep Convictions*.

Let me explain: *Deep Convictions* is specifically designed to help you delve into the Scriptures. It is set up to guide you as you learn to dig into the word of God and unearth insights on your own. Learning to do this is essential to your growth as a disciple. Nothing would trouble me more than learning that someone bypassed that kind of approach and just decided to let me spoon feed them through the thoughts in this book. Certainly, I will be referring to Scripture and quoting passages. I don't want to give you anything that is not grounded in God's truth. However, this book is not set up to encourage the important kind of investigation of Scripture that you will find in the earlier work.

If you have to make a choice, use the daily studies that you find in *Deep Convictions*. My greatest concern is that you and your Bible become great friends. Everything important I have learned about life, I learned there.

I would love to hear how these "letters" impact you. As a publisher, as well as a writer, I am always thinking about future editions. Your feedback will help us do something even better for the next generation of believers.

1
You Started a Party

Dear new disciples,

Let me start by telling you that I admire and respect you for the decision you recently made. You took the time to study carefully the teachings of the most radical revolutionary this world has ever known, and after looking at his message, you decided to follow him. Many people do not have the courage you have. You may not feel like some marvelously courageous person, but few have the guts to do what you have done. Most people are too worried about what someone else will think. They are too concerned about protecting something they have worked hard for. They are too afraid that Jesus Christ will not deliver as promised.

But you, my friends, stepped out of the crowd and stepped into Christ. You may have done so with some fear and some trepidation, but you did it! You did not let your fears hold you back. You did not let someone else's disapproval keep you from putting your faith in God's work. The Bible tells us,

> And without faith it is impossible to please God, because anyone who comes to him must believe that he exists and that he rewards those who earnestly seek him (Hebrews 11:6).

You and I both know that you have just begun and that you have a lot of growing to do. But you need to know that what you have done is pleasing to God and is encouraging to others, like me, who have been around for a long time. You did the right thing. You made the right choice, and the fact that it is not a popular choice makes it all the more unique. There will be many more times in your life when you will have to swim against the current of this world and go a different direction than the crowd, but you would not be a new Christian today had you not been willing to take that most difficult first step.

I know something about the people who studied the Bible with you. I know they taught you about the love of God, demonstrated at the cross where Jesus died. I know they told you that in Christ all your sins are forgiven. I know they taught you that becoming a disciple means entering into many blessings, including some of the best relationships you will ever have. But I also know they did not sugarcoat the message of Jesus for you. They told you the whole truth. They told you this would be the greatest challenge you have ever accepted. They told you there would be people who would persecute you because of this decision. They showed you that Jesus promised as much. And yet, after hearing the whole story, you said, "I want to make Jesus my Lord. I want to follow him. I want to be his disciple."

With that conviction you went into the water of baptism. In baptism you were buried with Christ and you were raised with him. That is what the Bible says happened (Romans 6:1-4). And when you came up out of that water, you started a party in heaven. Now, you might be saying, "But I have never even started a party on earth, how I could I have started a party in heaven?" But the truth is that you did! Sometime you should read Luke 15, and you will see what I am talking about. Your coming back to God sent shock waves through heaven and started a celebration that probably has not stopped yet. Read the passage carefully and you will see that not only do the angels rejoice, but also God himself. In fact, the last story in Luke 15 makes it clear that it is God the Father who starts the party.

You may say, "But I don't deserve such attention," and in one way you would be right. None of us deserves what God gives us. What we are talking about here is "grace." We will talk more about it later, but grace means that God gives us far more than we deserve and something we could never earn. We don't deserve such a celebration. We know ourselves too well. We know that it was our sin, not our goodness, that brought us to see our need for God. God certainly sees our sin. He is no grandfather in the sky who naively thinks we are all just wonderful and could do no wrong. But God also sees our value and our potential. Because of his grace, he offered us forgiveness and a new beginning, and now it causes him to rejoice and start a party when he sees us go against the world and accept his offer.

Have you ever seen pictures of one of the old-fashioned ticker-tape parades in New York City? The heroes ride through the streets and the people blow horns and shout compliments, and the ticker tape is poured out the windows of the buildings. It is a giant party in honor of someone. I want you to think about this for a while and let it soak in: Your response to

God, your determination to be a disciple, your decision to be baptized into Christ are huge things, and all heaven is celebrating your faith, your courage and your heart for God. They are having a giant party in honor of you. They know you aren't perfect. They know you will hit some bumps. They know you have a lot of growing ahead of you, but they are full of joy because you stepped up and stepped out of the crowd, and made the decision that God so much wants everyone to make.

So sit back and be amazed. Be amazed that God loves you the way he does. Be amazed that he forgives you as completely as he does. Think of someone in your life who brings you a lot of joy, and then be amazed that your life can bring God this kind of joy. When you came out of the water of baptism, my guess is that there were people there celebrating. They clapped. They sang. They hugged you. Be amazed that this was just a small celebration compared to the one going on in heaven in your honor.

2
Walking with God

Dear young disciples,

Just a few weeks ago I heard a man speak about walking with God—certainly a lost art in our world. We must understand that this Christian life is not about rituals, recognition, regimens or rules. It is about knowing God as a father, as a friend and as a guide. It is about giving him our lives and letting him give us his life.

Jesus Christ died for us. He is our Savior and our Redeemer. But what has he saved us from and what has he redeemed us for? He has saved us from separation from God, and he has brought us into a relationship where we can have fellowship with God every hour of every day. We were saved so we might enter into *and then enjoy* this relationship. And what a relationship it can be. (Don't forget that party!)

You do not read very far in the Bible before you see that this God who is talked about wants relationships. He values them. The Bible makes it clear that there is even relationship within God (between the Father, the Son and the Holy Spirit). From the earliest part of Genesis we see that God wanted a relationship with the man and the woman. This has always been what it is all about. Genesis 5:22 tells us about a man named Enoch who "walked with God" for many, many years. Walking with God means talking to God. It means listening to God. It means wanting to obey and please God. This particular man pleased God so much that finally God just took him on to heaven even before he died. God has an Enoch-type plan for us all. He wants us to walk with him here and then to continue our relationship with him forever. God is with you now, and God is with you forever.

I am sure that someone has already talked to you about how important it is that you have a "quiet time" every day. I hope you understand what this is all about. It is not about being able to say you did something. It is not about some kind of religious performance. It is not about a "Christian checklist." It is about having time just to be with God. It is about doing what Jesus did—withdrawing to lonely places so you can pray (Luke 5:16). It is about having time just to meditate carefully and deeply on the wonders of God and on the word of God (Psalm 119:15 and 48). Some people like to take a walk and just pray out loud (yes, in some neighborhoods that would draw some strange looks!). Others, like me, who don't walk so well, like to get in their cars and drive on winding country roads, looking at the creation and just pouring out their hearts to God. The Bible promises that God will "restore our souls," and I know if I do not personally get these kinds of times with God, my soul begins to suffer. A quiet time is not all there is to a walk with God, but it sure is a great beginning to a new day. The person who gets this kind of time with God is so much more likely to keep in step with God's Spirit.

I wish I did not have to tell you this, but somewhere along the line you will probably be like many others who have gone before you. You will start off in this new life with some excitement and some joy, but eventually you will face a very tough temptation. You will be tempted to see your Christian life as just a matter of crowding in a quick quiet time, rushing to make this meeting, trying to keep up with that activity, giving this money and doing what this or that leader has asked you to do. If you begin to view it that way, you will find yourself in a bunch of trouble. But, I am here to tell you that you don't have to give in to that temptation. I am here to assure you that if you find yourself going through the motions, that you can always get back to a genuine walk with God. You can stop and get time with God and just enjoy your relationship with him.

When I am tempted in the way I am describing, I find that one of the best things I can do is open to the Psalms and just let David's example remind me of what it means to have a friendship with God. Certain psalms stand out in my mind. For instance, Psalm 19 helps me to worship God because of the beauty of his creation and the wonder of his word. The way that psalm ends helps me to lay my life before him in surrender. Psalm 34 encourages me to express my fears and then move on to show faith that God can deliver me from them all. When I am feeling especially low, it is good for me to see that a godly leader like David also felt this way and to see how he worked through it with God. Psalms 6, 13, 38 and 42 are great examples of just being real with God in this way. Other psalms help me get my focus back on how much God cares for me and wants a relationship with me. These would include Psalms 18, 23 and 31.

When you really love someone and cherish a relationship with them, from time to time you will go with them to do something out of the ordinary. In just a few days I will be taking my wife out on a dinner cruise to celebrate a special day in our lives. From time to time you just need to take a half day or a day or maybe an overnight, and go do something very different with God. Go to a quiet spot by a lake, by the ocean, in the mountains or in the country. Spend some money if you have to in order to get there. God is worth it (Matthew 26:6-11). And then just take time to praise God, to sing, to weep before God, to pour out your deepest feelings, to petition God for guidance, to pray through all the most important things in your life, and to pray for various people you care about. Just spend time with God. Let him restore your soul. Obviously, to do something like this you have to make plans. But we are always planning something—a vacation, a hunting trip, a shopping spree. When we care enough, we find a way.

But please hear this: If spending time with God in any of these ways is not at all easy for you, if you feel awkward, uncomfortable or just a bit lost doing it, *let someone help you.* Do not say, "Well, I guess this part is just not something I'm good at." This is not a "part" you can afford to be without or just have in a minimal way. And hear this: If it is not something you feel that much need for, you probably need it the most. Walking with God is the heart and soul of being a disciple of Jesus. This is the engine that propels the entire boat. Never forget that. There is absolutely no substitute for taking the time and energy to walk daily with your Father.

3

Jesus Is Lord

Dear new disciples,

It has not been long since you stood before others and made your good confession. "Jesus is Lord," you said for all to hear. You had good reasons for believing that and for saying it, but it is still an astounding statement. Jesus—a man who lived 2,000 years ago—is your *Lord*. Jesus of Nazareth, the man who never ventured far out of Palestine, the man who was officially executed by the most prestigious government on earth is your Lord, your master, your king, your mentor, your coach, your boss. He is *the* authority in your life.

This concept is at the same time a seemingly wild, crazy notion *and* the most reasonable conclusion anyone has ever come to. There may be some days when your faith wavers, and you wonder if the truth is more in the "wild and crazy" direction. In reality, there has never been anyone like Jesus—no one who ever lived like he lived, no one who ever died with his purpose, and no one who ever came back from the dead, never to die again.

In your life as a Christian, you will experience many attacks. Your entrance into Christ may have started a party, but that party also sent you off to war as part of God's army. You are fighting for the greatest of causes. Every battle is one that is worth fighting. However, you will take some hits. There will be days when you give some thought to taking an easier road. This is where Jesus must come in. I am just one of the older disciples around who can tell you that the only reason I am still here is *Jesus*. There have been days when I wasn't sure I wanted to continue. There have been nights when I felt I just did not want to give anymore. There were times when leaders disappointed me, other disciples aggravated me and non-Christians were ungrateful for the help I was offering them. But Jesus always kept me coming back.

Jesus—thank God—just will not go away. After a frustrating night, he will still be there the next morning as you open and read the Gospels. After you have been hurt by your own failure, or by someone else's, he remains unchanged. He still knows more about life than anyone who ever lived. His words are still the ones you need. He still loves you. He still forgives you and others. He still calls for repentance. He still offers hope. If you are focused on Jesus, you will make it. Some other disciples may let you down or overlook your needs, but if you are focused on Jesus, you will make it. (And by "make it" I don't just mean "survive." I mean you will move through the challenges to live a fruitful, fulfilling life.)

Let me open your eyes: You will never, ever be in a perfect church. You will never, ever have perfect leaders. You will never have perfect disciplers or be a perfect disciple. Sorry, it is just not going to happen on this little terrestrial ball we call earth. However, if you stay with Jesus and keep your eyes on him, you will stay with one who is perfect, one who finished a perfect plan, one who brings perfect grace and one who has a perfect conclusion in store for all those who love him. And don't forget, even though the church, the leaders and your discipler are not perfect, Jesus is the One who is perfectly sure that you need them all.

Some time ago I decided to start every time with God in the morning by repeating the confession I made when I was baptized. When I repeat those words, "Jesus is Lord," it immediately gets me focused, clarifies my thinking and gives me fresh direction for a new day. It brings me back to the crucial issue. The issue is not *Did someone overlook me yesterday?* It is not *Did I get worn out trying to help someone?* It is not *Am I finding living a spiritual life to be challenging?* It is not even *Am I having fun?* The crucial issue is Jesus and my connection to him. Paul made this clear in his letter to the Colossians. Read his words very carefully. Speaking of Jesus, he writes:

> *He is the image of the invisible God, the firstborn over all creation. For by him all things were created: things in heaven and on earth, visible and invisible, whether thrones or powers or rulers or authorities; all things were created by him and for him. He is before all things, and in him all things hold together. And he is the head of the body, the church; he is the beginning and the firstborn from among the dead, so that in everything he might have the supremacy. For God was pleased to have all his fullness dwell in him, and through him to reconcile to himself all things, whether things on earth or things in heaven, by making peace through his blood, shed on the cross (Colossians 1:15-20).*

The crucial issue in my life today is *Will I allow Jesus, who created all things and who holds all things together, to direct me and control me and hold all things together for me?* Jesus is Lord. He is Lord of the cosmos. Keeping that clear in our minds is the most crucial issue.

When you chose to follow Jesus and to be his disciple, you did a very smart thing, and you made a very good decision. He knows you. He knows what you need. He knows how to get you where you need to go. He knows how to develop and mature your character. He will lead you with the love and compassion of a caring father, a tender mother and a gentle shepherd. The Bible uses all these images to talk about him. Best of all, he will never leave you. Just be sure you continually decide that you will never leave him.

Say it every day: "Jesus is Lord!"

4

Life with a Purpose

My new brothers and sisters,

In this new life you have chosen to live, you will have some great times. You will have some of the best experiences that a human being can have. But, of course, you will have some challenges. I am sure that none of you came into this thinking that it was all going to be the proverbial bed of roses. (Of course, if you had not chosen to follow Jesus, you would have had challenges, too—but without Jesus and fellow disciples to help you handle them.) Later I am going to write to you about some of the challenges that come in the spiritual life, but here I want to emphasize to you that whatever the difficulties may be, it is all worth it because you have now embraced a life with a purpose.

I am writing this letter as I sit in a cottage we have rented on a beautiful lake in New Hampshire. Across the way a man is working hard on the porch of his home. From the looks of his place, he spends hours keeping everything in great shape. I talked with him briefly when I was here in the past. He commutes into Boston four days a week, but lives for the weekends when he can get back to his place. He would quit his job tomorrow if he had enough money to retire. There are thousands of people like him whose major purpose in life seems to be building the right house in the right spot or getting the right car and keeping it in immaculate shape. There are others who seem to have no higher purpose than playing music, shopping or watching the latest sports event, movie or soap opera.

Sure there are some people who work hard to raise their kids and contribute something to their schools and their community. There are even some highly paid folks who get involved in activities to help the poor and the disadvantaged. Not everyone in the world lives a purely self-indulgent life-style. Some people have decided they must find a higher purpose.

But, young disciple, here is where you need to realize what you have. You have the highest of all purposes. You are now involved in living the most meaningful and significant life that a person can possibly live. Listen to Peter:

> But you are a chosen people, a royal priesthood, a holy nation, a people belonging to God, that you may declare the praises of him who called you out of darkness into his wonderful light (1 Peter 2:9).

As we have already seen, you are walking with God. You have a relationship with the Lord of the Universe. You are a chosen person and a part of a chosen community. When the dust settles, or, more accurately, when the last great firestorm is over (2 Peter 3:10-11), the work of many famous politicians will not matter; the songs sung by many top artists will not matter; the corporations built by some of the world's brightest businessmen will not matter. But everything you did as a disciple of Jesus will matter. Even the little cup of cold water you offered to some neglected soul in the name of Jesus will matter (Matthew 10:42).

As we have already seen, the crucial issue in this world is Jesus. Everything connected to him will endure. Everything without a connection to him will spoil, fade and perish. Things that seemed glorious and received the headlines and television coverage, will not matter. Only those things tied to Jesus are destined for immortality (2 Timothy 1:10).

And so consider your purpose. You are tied to Jesus and you have the opportunity and the ability to bring Jesus into the lives of more and more people. Someone brought Jesus into your life. And you are grateful. You have no trouble seeing that the people who helped you find him have a life full of purpose. They saved your life. That makes them pretty special and makes their lives count in a big way. Right? But now you have the same Jesus they have, and you can be used to share him; and that means you can be used to change eternity for others. Find a greater purpose than that one!

The person who finds a cure for AIDS, the person who stops a war and negotiates peace, the actor who inspires a country to look for a cure to spinal cord injuries and the woman who opens our eyes to the plight of the poorest of the poor all have done something worthwhile and commendable. But if you bring one friend to Christ, make them a disciple and teach them to help someone else become a disciple, you will have done something greater. You may not get a Nobel Prize, but you will save both yourself and your hearers (1 Timothy 4:16).

A friend of mine recently told some of us an amazing story. Nearly twenty years ago his young son fell through a plate glass window, severing an artery in his neck. The boy would have died within minutes had it not been for the presence of a fast-thinking off-duty police officer who had been trained in first aid. This man held his hand inside the boy's neck, stopping the blood flow all the way to the hospital. Once there, other emergency measures were taken, but his life was saved. My friend was so moved by the officer's efforts that he went to the police station shortly after the incident to volunteer to do anything they might need him to do.

Now a disciple, my friend told us that his experience has helped him see what a willing volunteer he needs to be in the kingdom of God. We should respond to all Jesus has done for us by gratefully volunteering to do anything for him. His response to our offer is to give us the greatest purpose known to man: to bring others to God.

You will have your challenges. You will have your trials. You may even have days when you wonder, *Is it worth it?* I have. But the answer clearly is "Yes, it is worth it." I remember at least a decade ago seeing the reports of an airliner that crashed in the Potomac River in Washington, DC. A man named Lenny was one of those standing near the bank on that icy day, and he was one of the first to plunge in to try to save those who were floating to the surface. He saved several lives and in countless interviews with TV reporters he expressed the same idea again and again. "It was worth it." It was cold. It was wet. It was dangerous. But it was worth it. When he got the phone calls from the grateful people and their grateful family members, he knew assuredly that it was worth it.

If you could find Lenny today, I am sure you would find he has not changed his mind. Talk with disciples who have been around for a while. Talk to those who have gone through some real hardships in their efforts to bring others to Christ. Ask them: Is it worth it? Don't just listen to what they say. Look in their eyes. Look down into their souls. You will realize that you are talking to people who have found the greatest purpose that can be found.

5

Hungering
Like Newborn Babies

Dear new disciples,

By the time you were old enough to understand conversation, you probably had an aversion to anyone calling you a baby. No self-respecting two-year-old appreciates that term when it is being used for him or her. But when you decided to become a Christian, you decided to get humble, so I am sure you will not mind me telling you that as a new disciple you are a baby. If you do feel offended, please keep in mind that this is how the Bible describes you. Writing to new Christians, Peter said, "Like newborn babies, crave pure spiritual milk, so that by it you may grow up in your salvation" (1 Peter 2:2).

Peter is not trying to make you feel unimportant or to ridicule you. He is just recognizing that you are like a baby in that you are at the beginning of a new life, and he wants you think about how babies stop being babies. He wants you to think about how they grow up. They do it by craving food, and if you have ever been around newborns, you know that they are not at all shy about letting you know that they want to eat.

Some friends of ours just had a baby. That new little girl cannot change the fact that she is a baby. Right now you are a baby Christian. You cannot change that fact any more than she can. But it is not God's plan for her to stay a baby, and it is not God's plan for you to stay a baby. But here is where you need to learn from baby Jillian. She can show you how to grow. She craves her mother's milk. She is intense about getting it. She acts like she is going to die if she doesn't get it. Are you getting the point?

You are a baby. Just admit it. It is not a problem. It is just where you are. If you are still a baby a year from now, that will be a problem. But right now, it is fine. *All you have to do is act like one.* Specifically, act like one when it comes to eating. What Peter is saying is that you need to hunger for spiritual milk—the basics of the word of God—just like little Jillian hungers for her mom's milk.

Now there is a difference between you and Jillian. No one has to tell her to be hungry. She came with that built in. Being a physical baby is all about natural instincts. Being a spiritual baby is all about a decision that you made and decisions that you have to keep making.

Originally, you made the decision to study the Bible. You made the decision to let someone teach you what they knew. Those were two good decisions. Then after you had learned many things, you were faced with the big decision. I don't know how long it took you to make it or what all you went through before you made it, but you made it. You decided that you need Jesus Christ and that you need him to be Lord of your life.

Unlike little Jillian, you decided you wanted to be born, and you responded with repentance and baptism. You were born again (1 Peter 1:23). With that decision, I expect there has come some natural desire to know more, but here is what I think Peter is saying to you: Just as you made a decision to become a Christian, *you must make a decision to be hungry as a Christian.* On certain days you may find your desire greater than on other days, but on all days you must make the decision to eat and eat heartily. Jillian's life depends on eating. She knows that instinctively. Your life as a disciple depends on eating well. You need to know that spiritually.

I have been involved with young Christians for many years. Some people are like Greg. They become disciples and then they do exactly what Peter says—they crave pure spiritual milk. They get serious about a daily quiet time. They get the Bible open every day. They take the study helps that are given to them, and they use them. They keep a journal. They write down what they are learning. They are eager to take notes on sermons and classes so they can study them later. They ask questions about things they do not understand. They change their habits. They watch less TV and stop wasting time in other ways. They look for ways to get more time in God's word and more time being taught the Scriptures. Can you guess what happens to people like this? They grow. They mature. They have an impact on others around them. Before long, some of them are being asked to lead others. They no longer look or act like babies. Greg grew up to be a strong man of God.

Others are like someone I know named James (not his real name). They make the biggest decision of their lives, but they don't act like they made it. They do not rearrange their priorities. They don't make the time every day to dig into God's word. They stay focused on other things and think that somehow this new thing of being a Christian can just be worked into the other things that are very important to them. They try to live off a few spiritual snacks. They enjoy the sermons and classes but think they will do fine as long as they are simply there to listen. Can you guess what happens to people like this? Let Jesus tell you about them:

> *"A farmer went out to sow his seed. As he was scattering the seed, some fell along the path; it was trampled on, and the birds of the air ate it up. Some fell on rock, and when it came up, the plants withered because they had no moisture"* (Luke 8:5-6).

> *"Those on the rock are the ones who receive the word with joy when they hear it, but they have no root. They believe for a while, but in the time of testing they fall away"* (Luke 8:13).

When you do not hunger for the Word, you do not grow; and when you do not grow, you stay weak and vulnerable. When you are weak and the time of testing comes, you do not make it. "James" did not make it, and if you follow in his steps, you will not make it either. The time of testing did come for him, as it comes for us all, and he was easy prey for the enemy because he had not filled himself up with truth. All around him were truth and wisdom. But he did not hunger, and he did not grow, and then he died.

But I join the writer of the book of Hebrews in saying: "Even though we speak like this, dear friends, we are confident of better things in your case—things that accompany salvation" (Hebrews 6:9). My prayer is that you will be a "Greg" and that you will go after the truth of God like a newborn baby goes after her mother's milk. Greg has made a huge difference in the lives of many people. I don't know how many people God will affect through you, but probably more than you can imagine. Just act like a baby!

6
Dealing with Sin

Dear new disciples,

I have some friends who are survivalists. They get a kick out of going into nearby mountains that are known to have some of the roughest weather in the world and spending a few days figuring out how to survive. To each his own! Not exactly my idea of a fun weekend. But I do learn a lot about life, and about spiritual life, when they tell me about their experiences.

They see these times as big adventures, but they know it could all turn to tragedy if they do not pay close attention to some of the dangers they face. Talking about the dangers does not take away their fun. They know that they have to honestly face these things and figure out how to overcome them, or there will be no fun at all.

In this letter, I want to talk with you about something dangerous. If you are tempted to jump to the next letter because you only like to talk about pleasant things, you will be making a big mistake. You did start a party (And I think I can hear the celebration in heaven still going on. They do things in a big way there!), but to keep the party going, you must be alert and know what to do when trouble strikes.

When you studied to become a disciple, you learned that human beings have one problem that is bigger than all other problems. That problem is sin. You learned that your sin separated you from God. You learned that Jesus is so important because he is the only one who can deal with sin. You felt great after your baptism because you understood that all of your sin had been forgiven and that you stood before God without blemish or accusation (Colossians 1:22). However, if you thought, *Great! Now I won't have to worry about sin again*, you thought wrong.

Being a Christian does not mean the end of sin in your life. It means the end of sin's tyranny. It means the beginning of a whole new and victorious approach to dealing with sin. But I have seen too many young Christians fall victim to the enemy (whom we will discuss in detail later), because they did not understand what the Bible says about our ongoing struggle against sin. I don't want you to be uninformed. That is why I am writing this letter.

The first thing you must understand is that sin is no longer an option for you. Sin is anything that goes against the will of God, which is no longer the way you are going. You may sin (we will talk about that shortly), but you must be dead set against sin. When you do sin, it should never be because you thought it was acceptable. Several passages from the letter to the Romans sum up the attitude the disciple must have toward sin:

What shall we say, then? Shall we go on sinning so that grace may increase? By no means! We died to sin; how can we live in it any longer? (Romans 6:1-2).

In the same way, count yourselves dead to sin but alive to God in Christ Jesus. Therefore do not let sin reign in your mortal body so that you obey its evil desires. Do not offer the parts of your body to sin, as instruments of wickedness, but rather offer yourselves to God, as those who have been brought from death to life; and offer the parts of your body to him as instruments of righteousness. For sin shall not be your master, because you are not under law, but under grace (Romans 6:11-14).

With terrorism now a worldwide problem, we hear a great deal about police bomb squads. Members of such squads may sometimes make mistakes in handling explosives, but their commitment is to do everything they can to avoid a mistake. They have zero tolerance for mistakes in their work. The same thing can be said of good airline pilots and doctors. It must be the same with a disciple. We must have zero tolerance when it comes to sin. We must realize that it always does damage. We must hate sin. We must oppose it. We must plan not to sin and pray that we will not sin.

That being the case, you must understand what sin is. You know some of the obvious things. You know that sexual immorality, drunkenness, lying, stealing and violence are sins. We must understand that other actions are sin, including self-ishness, speaking hurtful words, pride in its many and diverse forms, selfish ambition, anything that comes from putting yourself at the center of your thinking and anything that is contrary to love. The more you dig into God's word, the more you will learn, but even now you need a much greater under-standing than that of the typical religious person who thinks of sin only as "breaking the Ten Commandments." Like my friends who go to the mountains, you must clearly identify the dangers, or else you will become a victim to them.

But once you know what sin is and once you set yourself against it, you must face this fact: *You will still sin.* That is not a pleasant fact, but it is a fact. Spiritual groups that try to avoid this fact gravitate into all kinds of false doctrines. They end up with people pretending to be something that they are not. Leaders in these groups particularly are discouraged from being honest about their lives. They may even "redefine" sin so they don't feel guilty of it. The result is not pretty.

The Scriptures teach us something very different and combine an opposition to sin with an understanding of grace that is sorely needed. Listen to this example from the Apostle John:

> *My dear children, I write this to you so that you will not sin. But if anybody does sin, we have one who speaks to the Father in our defense—Jesus Christ, the Righteous One. He is the atoning sacrifice for our sins, and not only for ours but also for the sins of the whole world (1 John 2:1-2).*

John was no friend of sin. He hated it. He worked to keep it out of his life and the lives of others. He wrote this letter so that those who received it would not sin. "But," he told them, "if anybody does sin...." He clearly recognized that they would. He had even said earlier, "If we claim to be without sin, we deceive ourselves and the truth is not in us" (1 John 1:8).

John's message is not complicated. (1) We should be opposed to sin and make it our goal in life not to sin against God, man or ourselves. (2) When we fail to perfectly reach our goal, we should not give up because Jesus Christ is the Righteous One who has made atonement for our sins.

I spoke with someone recently who had made a decision to sin. After deciding to view pornography on the Internet, he then reasoned that there was no hope for him, and he plunged even more deeply into sins of sensuality and impurity. He decided that since he had already failed, he might as well fail totally. There was another road he could have taken. He could have stopped after the first sin and confessed that sin to God and to others (James 5:16, 1 John 1:7). He could have been forgiven right there and experienced a new beginning as the result of God's amazing grace. He did not have to give up and continue in sin.

You can find good discussions of this in other books, but here is my message to you: Hate sin. It wrecks lives, homes, marriages and relationships. Plan. Pray. Get all the help others can give you so that you will not sin. If one plan does not seem to be working, get help and get a new plan. However, if you do sin, do not give up. Give it back to God. Come humbly before him. Be broken over it (Psalm 51:17). Have "godly sorrow" about it (2 Corinthians 7:10-11). After all this, however, accept God's forgiveness. Rejoice in his grace. Marvel at his grace. Stand amazed at his grace. Then get up, and go after righteousness again with a grateful and determined heart.

1

Commitment to the Body

Dear brothers and sisters,

For many new disciples, one of the biggest changes in their new lives is the commitment they make to the body of Christ. I am, of course, talking here about commitment to the church (Colossians 1:24). In many cases, before we became disciples, we lived very independent lives. We were probably committed to a job because it was our livelihood. We may have been committed to an athletic team or a band for the love of sport or music. Those commitments somewhat restrained our lives, but we still made many decisions mostly on the basis of what we thought was good for us or what we wanted to do.

Now however, as disciples, we have made a commitment to Christ. This means we have made a commitment to that which he loves and died for—his church. We understand that we are not in this world just to please ourselves. We are here to advance his kingdom, build up his church and make her great. We are here to love the people in his church and do those things that are best for their spiritual growth. Listen to how Paul put it, first in Romans 12, and then in Romans 15:

> ...so in Christ we who are many form one body, and each member belongs to all the others (Romans 12:5).

> Be devoted to one another in brotherly love. Honor one another above yourselves (Romans 12:10).

> We who are strong ought to bear with the failings of the weak and not to please ourselves. Each of us should please his neighbor for his good, to build him up. For even Christ did not please himself (Romans 15:1-3a).

It is clear from passages like these and many others that once we are in the kingdom we have a higher calling. We are to be devoted to others because we now understand that we belong to others.

For many of us this represents a major shift in thinking, and this concept will test us severely. We all struggle with selfishness. We all have tendencies to put the needs of others on the back burner. But now we understand that the greatest life comes from losing ourselves for the good of Christ, his church and others.

One of your first tests may come when you wake up some Sunday morning and don't feel very motivated to get dressed and go to church. Some of you will think back to your college days and recall that it did not hurt that much to miss an occasional class, and you reason that the same is probably true of church. But there is a major difference. It is unlikely you had made a commitment to the other members of your science or history class. Everyone was there doing his or her own thing. But now, you are part of a team that has a major task to accomplish. You need the encouragement of others, but much more than that, you need to be there to give of yourself to others. (One of the worst mistakes too many young Christians make is to think of church as more of a time to get than as a time to give.) At every stage of our Christian lives, we all have something to contribute and we all need to be there to let God use us to build up the whole body.

Envision a scenario I have seen played out with variations a number of times. A disciple decides he does not want to be with the church today. He thinks it will only affect him. He, of course, is wrong. The person who disciples him is affected, and that affects this brother's wife. The couple leading his "family group" are most concerned about him—knowing some of his patterns from the past. They have to fight off discouragement to give to others and need some help from those who disciple them. The service is a large one with hundreds in attendance, but many members of our group miss him and feel let down by not having him there as we make a great effort to influence others to see the power of Christ's church.

All of this distress could have been avoided if our independent brother had sincerely asked one simple question: "What would God want me to do?" (And that is a question that will serve you well in situation after situation. Learn to ask it with an open heart and an open mind.) But let's give this brother the benefit of the doubt and say that something very emotionally difficult was going on and that he just did not know how to give to others in that state. He still could have called for help. He still could have said, "I want to be there to give to others, but I am struggling with something. Can you help me get my bearings?" But on many occasions the people making this decision give no indication of wanting to give to others. That is precisely the attitude that you cannot have as a disciple.

Being devoted to Christ means being devoted to that to which he is devoted. Being a disciple of his means following in his steps and laying your life down for that for which he laid down his life:

> *Husbands, love your wives, just as Christ loved the church and gave himself up for her to make her holy, cleansing her by the washing with water through the word (Ephesians 5:25-26).*

Jesus loved the church and he still loves the church. He gave himself up for her to make her great. As his disciple, one of your deepest convictions must be to love his church, to sacrifice for his church, to build up his church. Selfish decision making must die. Truly, in losing your life for his sake, you find it.

8
Eager
For Discipling

Dear young disciples,

    In my next three letters to you I want to talk more about one of the most important aspects of your new life: your relationships with other disciples. You have come into a new relationship with God, but even a quick reading of the New Testament shows you that God wants you to have a new set of relationships with those who are your brothers and sisters in the faith.

    In this letter I want to speak with you about the whole issue of "being discipled." I am sure that some-one studied Matthew 28:18-20 with you before you made your decision to be baptized, but let's look at it again:

> *Then Jesus came to them and said, "All authority in heaven and on earth has been given to me. Therefore go and make disciples of all nations, baptizing them in the name of the Father and of the Son and of the Holy Spirit, and teaching them to obey everything I have commanded you. And surely I am with you always, to the very end of the age."*

This passage is very important for many different reasons. You will likely hear it talked about often. But for now, notice that after someone makes the decision to be a disciple, they need to be taught (by someone else) to obey everything that Jesus commanded to the original group of disciples. Jesus' plan from the very beginning was for us to have relationships in the kingdom of God where we can be taught more and more about what it means to follow him. It was never his plan for people to become Christians, take their Bibles, and go figure out on their own how to live this life.

You can see later in the letters of Paul that he clearly understood the role we are to play in each other's lives. Look at this passage from Colossians 3:16:

> *Let the word of Christ dwell in you richly as you teach and admonish one another with all wisdom, and as you sing psalms, hymns and spiritual songs with gratitude in your hearts to God.*

All disciples need people in their lives who care about them, who care about God's will and who will teach and admonish them *with all wisdom*. There are no exceptions to this need, and there is never a time in life when it stops being a need. As you look around, you will see some very strong leaders in the kingdom. Please understand two things. (1) They got this way because they were willing to let others teach and admonish (that is "disciple") them. (2) They still need people in their lives to disciple them. Though they are strong, they still need to grow and change, and they need discipling relationships in order to do that, just as you do.

But now I want to give you some very important advice: Have a great attitude about being discipled by others. Over the years I have seen how quickly some people have matured after becoming Christians and how slowly others have matured. Usually the difference is found right here. Those who recognize how much others can help them and who are eager to be discipled are the ones who grow rapidly. Those who are resistant to discipling are the ones who grow slowly, if at all.

Quite often in the Bible, the Christian is compared to an athlete, and athletic images are used to help us understand things we need to be or do. One of the keys for success in athletics is to be very open to coaching. As I write this, a young American golfer has burst onto the scene possessing a level of skill and power perhaps like no one else who has ever played the game. His spectacular play has revolutionized interest in golf around the world. However, just recently I read an article about the man he has hired as his personal coach, and how strongly he feels about having this coach continue with him. This athlete is already among the world's elite, but he knows he needs someone outside himself, observing him and giving him input. If he ever becomes arrogant and foolish enough to think he can be his own coach, you can be sure his performance will drop off dramatically.

These principles here are so important for disciples. By our very nature, we are limited in how much we can see, evaluate and teach ourselves. Sure, the Bible does tell us, "Train yourself to be godly" (1 Timothy 4:7), and we should be doing everything we can to grow. But "everything we can" involves building strong relationships like those described in Scripture in which we can get advice, correction, counsel, teaching, admonishment, encouragement and even at times, rebukes (2 Timothy 3:16-4:2).

In your relationships with others in the church you will have one of two attitudes. You will either believe "I need all the help I can get, and I am eager to get it" or you will believe "I can think for myself. I don't really need all these people trying to show me what to be." The first person described here may not always get the best advice, the best counsel or the best discipling. Those working with him will make some mistakes; but his attitude is the right one and the one God can bless. He will learn and he will grow and he will become a joy in the kingdom. He is fundamentally humble, and God blesses humility. The second person is fundamentally proud. He is also foolish. The book of Proverbs bluntly says that he is stupid (Proverbs 12:1 NIV). He has come into what we might even call "the kingdom of humility" (the place where humility is to be the primary attitude), and he is trying to make it without humility in his relationships. That is stupid.

I pray that as you read these words, there is no doubt in your heart about which kind of person you are going to be. But if you are struggling with being humble—and many of us have struggled with it—let me give you just a bit more encouragement. I am not talking here about giving up your own mind and just turning your life over to the direction of others, as some critics of discipling portray. What I am talking about is getting in touch with the truth. The truth is that all of us need to learn a lot more about how to walk with God, how to love, how to be a spouse, how to be a parent, how to be a child, how to be a friend, how to be a person of integrity on the job and how to shine like a star in many other situations. The truth also is that everyone can benefit from coaching, from input and from counsel when it comes from those who care about us and who have valid insight. When you get in touch with these truths and you follow them, you know the truth and the truth sets you free.

You will never, ever lose by being eager to be discipled, but you will lose a lot, possibly even your soul, by being resistant to it. Mistakes have been made by all those who have discipled me, but I am far, far better off because of discipling. You will never have a perfect discipler, but you will move toward perfection by being eager to be discipled (Colossians 1:28-29).

9
Resolving Conflicts

Dear brothers and sisters,

Conflict is something we are all used to in culture and in family, but somehow, when young Christians experience it in the church, it often knocks them for a loop. I am writing this to prepare you for times of conflict and to help you see that such times can become opportunities for God to work.

When we become Christians, we do so after learning that the church is a very different place from the world. We come into the kingdom rightfully expecting that people are going to have different attitudes, treat each other better and in general, have a deeper quality of relationships. Whenever people are following the scriptural teachings about relationships, all these expectations are realized.

However, this does not mean that there will be no problems, and we have to get used to that truth. I am sure that there were some problems to be dealt with on board Noah's ark. But it was still much better to be on the inside than on the outside! It is the same with the church. I'll take the problems on the inside any day. I have been out in the world. I don't want to be there again.

The big difference between the church and the world is not that we don't have conflicts (Acts 15:39, Philippians 4:2-3). The big difference is that we have godly principles for resolving those conflicts and going on to better things. It is these principles that you must learn.

Sometimes conflicts are the result of a difference in opinion, or at least that is where they start. In such cases, what is needed is continued communication (which involves more listening than talking—see James 1:19), humility and patience (see Ephesians 4:2). Many conflicts are resolved when people get more information and understand better where another person is coming from. The greatest danger here is jumping to conclusions, assigning motives to other people and making judgments about them before you have all the facts.

While differing opinions often start conflicts, most conflicts eventually involve some sin that must be dealt with in a biblical way. This is where we have such an advantage over the world. We call sin by its right name, and we deal with it in a godly way. This healthy, biblical approach to dealing with sin enables us to resolve conflicts that in the typical family, workplace or neighborhood may go on for years.

If you believe that someone has sinned against you, and you can be sure that in our imperfect churches someone will, the Bible spells out the course of action that you are to take. You may be a little fearful about this, but please realize that the unity of the church is always at stake in such situations, and that is a very big thing indeed. (Just read Ephesians 4:1-6 to see the importance of unity.) Also realize that God is totally behind every effort you make to resolve matters and be unified. Here is what Jesus told us to do:

> *"If your brother sins against you, go and show him his fault, just between the two of you. If he listens to you, you have won your brother over. But if he will not listen, take one or two others along, so that 'every matter may be established by the testimony of two or three witnesses.' If he refuses to listen to them, tell it to the church; and if he refuses to listen even to the church, treat him as you would a pagan or a tax collector" (Matthew 18:15-17).*

If you believe someone has sinned against you—treated you in an unrighteous way or misrepresented you in some way—then Jesus is very clearly telling you to go to them and explain your feelings. It should go without saying that you should go in love and with humility and gentleness yourself. I have known situations where someone huffed in to confront someone with sin, only to find out in the course of the conversation that they did not have all the facts and that the person had not sinned against them. If you explain what you feel and get the other person's point of view, you will be in a better position to bring them whatever truth they need to hear. If they confess and ask for your forgiveness, the matter is resolved, and it never needs to go further. In such a case, you need to completely forgive them and not bring that problem up again. Jesus says that you have won the other person over. In other words, you are back together, united for the same cause.

One extra word of encouragement is in order. I know the way many new Christians think. They realize that they are the babies in the family. They know that others have been around a lot longer than they have. They may think someone has sinned against them, but they doubt whether anyone will believe them or they doubt whether they are right in the matter. Probably the toughest situation is one that involves a leader whom they feel has wronged them (and we will deal with that more in the next letter). Often intimidated by some of these thoughts, they try pushing the issue under the rug or, as we often say, they try "stuffing it." They just hold it in and hope it will get better. Please learn this rule: *Anything stuffed eventually comes out.* And if it comes out after being stuffed for a long time, it will be smellier and uglier than ever. Even if you have doubts about how correct you are, it is much better to go ahead and talk with the person. When new disciples give in to their fears and stuff the feelings they have, it is not unusual to hear one day that they are no longer around. There was never an ugly eruption. They just left, unable to deal any longer with unresolved feelings or conflict in relationships.

One final comment before we look at the other side of the coin: If you do go to someone and they do not give you a fair hearing, or if they dismiss the matter and put it all back on you, this is where Jesus' second directive comes in. He says your next step is to ask two or three others to sit down with you and the person who has wronged you. You don't want to choose people who you just think will agree with you, but you want to ask wise, spiritually minded, objective people to help you and the other person sort out the issues.

If, the first time you try any of this, the person who has hurt you gives you a stinging response, you may be tempted to think, *That's it. I tried. I'm not taking this any further. This hurts too much.* That is when it is important to remember that Jesus is Lord, and you are not in this to feel comfortable and do what is easy. We are all in this to please him and keep unity in the kingdom. Obviously, if you get an unkind response from the other disciple, there is sin in the body that needs to be dealt with, and God is going to use you to help deal with it. Be faithful. Be of good courage. And don't give up.

The other side of the coin is that a conflict may exist because you have sinned against another person. We all have moments when we look back over something that happened, and we see in retrospect that we did not handle the situation in the right away. We realize that we blew it. But some of us don't do that much reflecting, and we march on, unaware of the people who have been left in our wake. In such cases, the word sometimes drifts back to us that this brother or this sister felt injured by something we did, or perhaps the person we injured comes back and tells us. In whatever way the realization comes, Jesus tells us what we should do:

> *"Therefore, if you are offering your gift at the altar and there remember that your brother has something against you, leave your gift there in front of the altar. First go and be reconciled to your brother; then come and offer your gift"* (Matthew 5:23-24).

Speaking to a Jewish audience still under the old covenant, Jesus pictured a situation where a Jew was coming to worship in the temple and there remembered that another person felt that he (the worshiper) was in the wrong in their relationship. It is most interesting that Jesus does not say, "You should resolve that situation and get it right with him as soon as you finish your worship." No, he gives instruction to put down the gift to be offered, to go outside the temple and back into the city, to find the person and get it resolved. Jesus counsels such an inconvenient course of action, no doubt, to make the point that getting things worked out with your brother is crucial to keeping things worked out with your God.

While most conflicts in the kingdom are resolved quickly, there will be exceptions. When you hit those exceptions and something does not get immediately worked out, keep your heart soft, do not stop praying, and do not stop working on the relationship. It is the only way for us to keep the kingdom united. In the family of God we will have conflicts, but with the help of God they can always be resolved.

10

Working with Leaders

Dear fellow Christians,

We all come into the kingdom of God with different experiences on our "life" resumes. Some of us had very good experiences with leadership, and others of us had very negative experiences. Some of us had great parents and many good teachers or coaches. Others of us may have felt harshness, disrespect and prejudice in our interactions with leaders. Whatever has happened to us in the past comes trailing along behind us in various ways when we enter into Christ. Our sins were forgiven, but all of our memories were not erased.

If we do not have good feelings about people in leadership, we have some work to do, because leadership is a key element in the kingdom of God. Having a good relationship with those who have leadership roles is a crucial need in the life of every Christian.

I know some people who have been so burned by poor leadership that they feel the best scenario would be a leaderless church situation. But nothing great ever gets done without leadership. Had it not been for the leadership of Abraham Lincoln, the United States might never have survived the Civil War. Had it not been for the leadership of Winston Churchill, the outcome of World War II might have been quite different. Without the leadership of Martin Luther King, many crucial changes in American culture would have at least been long delayed. Whether you are talking about the local Boy Scout troop or a diplomatic mission to China, leadership is always crucial. And leadership is a vital topic in the church of Jesus Christ.

In the last twenty-five years we have seen the kingdom of God advance around the world in unprecedented ways. Strong, godly, humble and spiritual leadership has been a key reason it has happened. Of course, it is God who makes things grow, but from Moses to Elijah to Isaiah to John the Baptist to Jesus to Peter and Paul, he made things grow in biblical times by blessing effective leadership, and that is still the way he works today.

The New Testament has more than a few things to say about how important leaders are and how important it is to work with them. Listen to these statements:

Now we ask you, brothers, to respect those who work hard among you, who are over you in the Lord and who admonish you (1 Thessalonians 5:12).

Remember your leaders, who spoke the word of God to you. Consider the outcome of their way of life and imitate their faith (Hebrews 13:7).

Obey your leaders and submit to their authority. They keep watch over you as men who must give an account. Obey them so that their work will be a joy, not a burden, for that would be of no advantage to you (Hebrews 13:17).

It is obvious that God has put spiritual leaders in place for some very important reasons. He has given them serious, and often sobering, responsibilities. They will have to give him an account of how they led those under their charge. But what is clear from these texts is that the basic attitude of every disciple toward leadership is to be a positive and supportive one. That does not mean you should never ask questions or give input; it does mean there is no place in the kingdom for the critical spirit who picks at actions, second-guesses decisions, or resists directions that are given.

Consider the admonitions in the passages above. In a world where disrespect abounds, disciples are to show respect for their leaders, for the task God has assigned them and for the hard work that has qualified them to lead. Nothing bothered me more as a parent than seeing my children act disrespectfully toward leaders, and nothing bothers me more in the church than seeing disciples treat leaders with disrespect. Show disrespect for God's leader, and you are showing disrespect for God. Such behavior disregards his clear command. More than just respecting a leader's "position," disciples are to appreciate the faith and spiritual qualities that caused people to be put in leadership. They are to observe the impact a spiritual life has, and they are to imitate their faith.

Finally, disciples are to be submissive to those in authority. Submission is such a broad and important concept for those who follow Jesus. When you study passages like Philippians 2:1-10 and 1 Peter 2:18-25, you realize that Jesus modeled submission, which means that God, incredibly, is a submissive God.

I urge you to carefully study the material on this topic in our earlier book *Deep Convictions*. Work carefully through all the passages. Submission needs to characterize your life, and it particularly needs to show up in your relationships with leaders.

Would you want to be in an army going into battle if you were not confident that the other soldiers were going to be submissive and obedient to the leaders? What chaos could result! Would you feel confident going in for open heart surgery if you heard that the medical support staff was often disobedient and disrespectful toward the chief surgeon? I have been a part of churches whose members were disrespectful toward their leaders and who had no convictions about being supportive and submissive to them. I thank God that I have not been in such a church for a long time. I pray I will never have to be in another one like that. It is an ugly thing to behold.

We have already, in earlier letters, noted that your leaders are not perfect and that you will never find any who are. If they sin, and they will, you will need to talk with them, as we said in the chapter before. If resolving things with any disciple is important, it is even more important to resolve things with leaders. But, whatever you do, do not allow the imperfections or mistakes of leaders to cause you to "throw the baby out with the bath water." The fact that leaders make mistakes does not justify a critical spirit toward leadership. We must not do away with parenthood because some parents foul up. We must also not undermine leadership because some leaders fail at some point.

In closing this letter, I want to remind you that God has given leaders some demanding challenges. Theirs is not a position of privilege, power and prestige. It is a position of great responsibility. To the leaders in the church at Ephesus Paul spoke these words:

Keep watch over yourselves and all the flock of which the Holy Spirit has made you overseers. Be shepherds of the church of God, which he bought with his own blood. I know that after I leave, savage wolves will come in among you and will not spare the flock. Even from your own number men will arise and distort the truth in order to draw away disciples after them. So be on your guard! Remember that for three years I never stopped warning each of you night and day with tears (Acts 20:28-31).

Peter closed out his first letter with some strong words to leaders:

To the elders among you, I appeal as a fellow elder, a witness of Christ's sufferings and one who also will share in the glory to be revealed: Be shepherds of God's flock that is under your care, serving as overseers—not because you must, but because you are willing, as God wants you to be; not greedy for money, but eager to serve; not lording it over those entrusted to you, but being examples to the flock. And when the Chief Shepherd appears, you will receive the crown of glory that will never fade away (1 Peter 5:1-4).

And, of course, it was Jesus himself who spoke the strongest words to aspiring leaders:

Jesus called them together and said, "You know that the rulers of the Gentiles lord it over them, and their high officials exercise authority over them. Not so with you. Instead, whoever wants to become great among you must be your servant, and whoever wants to be first must be your slave—just as the Son of Man did not come to be served, but to serve, and to give his life as a ransom for many" (Matthew 20:25-28).

Leaders carry a great weight. No one is given a greater challenge in the Bible than those who lead. But leaders are to accept their responsibilities joyfully and willingly. And you can help them to do that. You can make their load lighter. Get to know them. Let them get to know you. Initiate with them. Sure, they are busy, but you are their business. Take some of their time. Resolve conflicts with them when needed, and be there to help make their work a joy. That will end up being good for you, for them and for the whole body of Christ.

11

God Is in Control

Dear friends,

I cannot remember when I first heard someone say, "God is in control," but I can remember when I first started spending time with people who really believed that. The more I thought about that statement, the more I decided it contained one of the most powerful thoughts in the world—a thought capable of radically changing the way we look at so many situations.

You will probably not be in the kingdom very long before you hear people using this phrase. You may hear that someone has been diagnosed with a serious illness, and then you will hear someone say, "But God is in control." You may learn that missionaries to a certain country have been kicked out by a hostile government, and you will hear someone say, "But God is in control." Someone will tell you how he and his girlfriend have decided to end their dating relationship, and you will hear them both say, "But God is in control."

As I write this letter, we have received the news that a disciple in her thirties has died suddenly from an epileptic seizure. Her death has shocked all who knew her, but we will remind each other that "God is in control."

If you are the skeptical type, you may think this is a catch phrase that everyone uses to ease the pain when they don't understand what is going on. I suppose it could be used that way, but I feel confident that most of the people who I know really believe it. Yes, we probably tend to think more about it at those moments when plans do not work out as expected. Those times push us to think most deeply about the fact that there is a larger purpose, and there is Someone ultimately in control who is beyond us and over us.

The Bible communicates the message that God is in control from beginning to end. In Genesis we find a God who created the world out of nothing, who had a plan already in place when man sinned and fell, who purged the world with a flood when evil reigned and who preserved the seed line of the Messiah. In Exodus we find a God who was undeterred by the greatest power on earth and left the Pharaoh and his Egyptian people wondering what hit them. In the rest of the Old Testament we find a God who was disappointed again and again by the behavior of his people, but a God who never lost control. He brings blessings on those who obey him and curses on those who rebel against him. He always has a way to keep things moving toward the fulfillment of his plan.

In the New Testament we learn that when the time was perfect, Jesus came (Galatians 4:4). Because God was in control he did not come too soon or too late, but when the time was just right. The way conditions in the Roman Empire were so conducive to the spread of Christianity helps us see that God knew exactly what he was doing. Even on the darkest day in history, God was in control. The sinless Son of God was treated as a criminal, and he died horribly. But Peter would later assure the crowd on Pentecost that God was at work in it all. God did not do the evil or cause the evil, but God took the evil and used it for good. He never lost his grip. The last book of the Bible, written in the middle of a terrible persecution of the church, literally rings with the message that though nations rise and fall, God's people will live and reign forever.

It is important to note that the biblical writers, while they saw God in control of the great events of history, were equally convinced that God was in control of the everyday lives of his people. He is not a God who pulls off a flood, and then hundreds of years later an exodus, and then more than a thousand years later a resurrection, and simply rests in between. He is the God who is always working (John 5:17). He is the God who knows every sparrow that falls to the ground and has the hairs of our heads numbered (Matthew 10:29-30). He is at work in the big events and in the smallest of details. Paul puts it this way: "And we know that *in all things* God works for the good of those who love him, who have been called according to his purpose" (Romans 8:28, emphasis added).

In all things. Just think about that. You don't get the job you had hoped for. *In all things.* You get chronically ill. *In all things.* You break up with the person you thought for sure you would marry. *In all things.* One of your children is born with a serious birth defect. *In all things.* You do get the job you wanted. *In all things.* Your health remains excellent. *In all things.* You do marry the person of your dreams. *In all things.* Your children are born very healthy and without problems. *In all things.*

Do you understand what the Bible is saying? *In all things* God is at work. He works in what we call the "good," and he works in what we call the "bad." He works everything for the good of those who love him. He never loses control. He never says, "I did not anticipate this. What do we do now?" He never says, "Oops, I forgot about that." He doesn't bat .500. He doesn't bat .990. He bats 1.000. He never strikes out. Nothing in your life ever happens that he can't use for his good purposes. If you really get that idea into your heart and into your mind, it changes a lot of things. You just cannot be anxious when you hold to that conviction. You just cannot be frantic or insecure, if that is your faith. These are the reasons why I say it is one of the most powerful truths in the world.

If a leader sins in a way that affects many, that is bad; but God is still in control, and all is not lost. He can turn it into something good. If someone mounts a massive campaign of persecution against the church, that hurts; but God is still in control. We see in the pages of the New Testament that it was just such a campaign that God used to spread the gospel out of Jerusalem and move it on to Antioch in Syria and beyond. If a church building burns to the ground just when a congregation is about to move in, God has a better plan, and some who have been around longer can tell you some amazing stories about that.

I am not suggesting to you that as a Christian you should never grieve over something or feel hurt or a sense of loss. I am, however, suggesting that the grief should not go on and on. As a disciple you can get your bearings and focus on the omnipotent, sovereign God who never for a moment loses his grip on the lives of any of his children.

God is in control. *In all things.* In *all* things.

Believing that totally changes your life.

12
The Enemy

My friends,

Because it is always better to know the truth than to hide your head in the sand, I must write to you about the enemy. I am talking here, of course, about the devil—a.k.a. Satan (Matthew 13:39, Luke 10:19, 1 Peter 5:8). I wish I could tell you that you need never bother with him again, but that is just not the case. I wish I could tell you that when you came up out of the waters of baptism that he marked your name off his hit list, but what really happened is that he marked your name with his yellow highlighter. You really got his attention with that act. That is the bad news. But the good news is that, if you are prepared, you have at your disposal all you need to defeat him. The key phrase is *if you are prepared*.

First, let me acknowledge a question that you may have asked, but one which we cannot fully answer. That question is "Why does God allow the enemy to exist and to exercise power at all?" If we could answer that question, I am not sure it would help us. Sure, inquiring minds want to know, but there are some things we don't get to know. That is not the same as saying there is not an answer. In God's spiritual economy there are many things for which he has good reasons, but either I don't need to know what they are, or my pea-sized brain is just not big enough to understand them. I suspect that the enemy's continued existence at this stage of history has something to do with the free will that God has given to us all and the choices that are available to us to do right or to do wrong—but I won't pretend to have it all figured out.

I am more like the man who comes home and is told that there is a large poisonous snake in his bedroom, curled up on his bed. His first concern is not to figure out how the snake got there or why God would create a snake in the first place. His first concern is to find out how to get rid of it. Later on, he can work on the other issues, if he is still interested. I am like this man because I am told by the most credible and reliable person in human history that I have an enemy who wants to see my soul and my body destroyed in hell. I am told that this enemy is real, not a fairy tale or comic book character. I am told he has massive spiritual powers only exceeded by God himself. I am told he is scheming to pull me away from God and away from life.

If I spend my time arguing with God about why he would allow the enemy to exist, I am probably playing right into the bad guy's hands. My concern right now in the heat of the battle is to find out how to beat this enemy. Later on, when the battle is over and his head is cut off, or more accurately when he is thrown into a lake of fire, then I can ask some of the more philosophical questions, if I still care.

No one has all the answers about the devil, but this much is true: *The Bible tells us all we need to know to defeat him.* What more could we ask?

And so what does the Bible tell us about him?

We can only touch the basic outline here. If you would like to do more reading about the enemy (and you should), I would recommend *The Lion Never Sleeps* by Mike Taliaferro. Mike wrote this book especially for older Christians who are discipling younger Christians like you, but there is much in this short but powerful exposé of Satan's power for any reader. *The Screwtape Letters* by C.S. Lewis has also helped many people understand how the enemy works.

For our purposes let me call your attention to three facts.

(1) *The enemy is a schemer.* One of our earliest introductions to him is in the book of Job where he is scheming to destroy Job's faith and character. Later in 2 Corinthians 2, Paul talks about Satan's efforts to outwit us and take us through his schemes (v. 11). All of this says to me that he does not try to work us away from God with formulas and canned ideas. No, he analyzes us carefully and tailors his approach to our weaknesses and our vulnerabilities. He would not get very far by having a drug dealer move in next door to me. I would not be tempted to become a customer. That might, however, be a real scheme of Satan to reach some of you reading this book. With me, on the other hand, he would be much more likely to try to discourage me through a flare-up of my chronic illness or through an effort to get me to be prideful about my years around the kingdom. He might also try to accuse me of all the ways I fail to measure up.

All of this means we need to know ourselves well and have others around us who know us well. That kind of knowledge will help us identify the kinds of schemes the Chief Schemer will use so we can recognize his attacks for what they are.

(2) *The devil never makes us do anything.* Years ago a well-known TV show featured a comedian by the name of Flip Wilson. He became famous for the line, "The devil made me do it." It was popular comedy, but bad theology. As powerful as the enemy is, as many forces as he may bring to help tempt you, he cannot compel you to do anything. He can only tempt. He can tempt in clever ways, but he can only tempt. I am talking about what the enemy can do to Christians. I am aware that there are those who have completely given themselves over to the devil to do his will. But even those people can still escape his trap through the power of Christ (2 Timothy 2:26). So never fall for one of Satan's greatest schemes—getting us to plead that we are just victims, unable to do anything about our sin.

(3) *In every situation God will always give us the strength and the power to say "no" to the enemy's schemes, temptations and accusations.* The armor of God is great enough to resist the enemy's attacks (Ephesians 6:11). Satan can be successfully repelled with faith (1 Peter 5:8-9). Jesus Christ destroys the devil's work (1 John 3:8). God is fully capable of crushing Satan under his feet (Romans 16:20).

We would be foolish to laugh about the enemy. He is a serious being with a serious agenda. He is a terrorist and a liar and a false accuser. He will stoop to anything. He is like a madman holed up in a house. He knows he is ultimately going to die, but he wants to take as many people out as possible. He has you in his sights. Without God you are an easy target. With the help of God you can resist him, defeat him and overcome his evil with good.

13
Knowing Yourself

Dear forgiven friends,

In my last letter I wrote to you about the enemy and how he designs his schemes to fit our particular weaknesses and vulnerabilities. With that in mind, this is probably a good time to talk to you about the importance of knowing yourself. Many people keep making the same mistakes over and over and keep falling into the same traps because they really do not know themselves very well.

Years ago, I heard someone put all people into two categories. Obviously, there is oversimplification here, but generally I think his comment was very helpful. The two categories were (1) the accused and (2) the excused. Once we talk about these, I think you will see that you tend toward one or the other. Understanding which way you tend will be a big help in your walk with God.

Accused people are those who frequently feel guilty. They tend to be perfectionists and never quite think they measure up. They take responsibility when things go wrong in a group; they feel it must have been their fault. They have trouble believing that God has forgiven them. They are easily convicted of sin and their need to change, but they have trouble believing that they can change. They are usually hard working, conscientious and concerned about integrity; but they have a tendency to doubt their own abilities, their own motives and their own worth. They are generally more sensitive, but also more prone to depression and self-pity. They may also have more of a tendency to have doubts about God (then, of course, they feel guilty about that).

Excused people, on the other hand, have trouble seeing that they did anything wrong. They are quick to make "excuses" for their behavior. They have to be hit on the head with a two-by-four to see their sin (I hope you know I am speaking figuratively!). They tend to be people who take action, but do not spend much time thinking about what they do. The up side is that they do not get bogged down in a lot of analysis. They do not tend to be depressed. Integrity is not a natural concern of theirs; they are more focused on getting things done. They don't usually doubt themselves, but they tend to be insensitive, and generally do not have a clue that they have hurt someone else by their actions. In fact, when confronted by the hurt party, they have trouble believing that something they did could have been wrong. It is not easy for these people to feel broken over their sin. They are much better at seeing the sins of others than their own. In both types of personalities there are strengths and weaknesses. The enemy wants to diminish the strengths and exploit the weaknesses.

Which of these do you tend to be—accused or excused? Only a few people fit perfectly into one category, but I believe we all have a tendency in one direction or the other. For example, I am much more in the accused category, but there are some things about the excused personality that show up in my character. When I think about these categories in relation to people in the Bible, I suspect that Sarah, Jacob, King Saul, Jonah and Peter were all more naturally "excused" personalities. Jezebel, without question, also belongs on this list. I would guess that Gideon, David, Jeremiah, Thomas, Timothy, and maybe John the apostle, were more the "accused" types. (Paul, as a natural man, seems to have had the best and worst of both.) Sure, I am only speculating about the biblical characters, but I think there is something useful here for us to think about. When we understand our natural tendency, we have a hand up on the enemy. When we know ourselves well, we can take action to protect ourselves from attack.

Let me be more specific. Let's suppose that you conclude, with some counsel from others, that you tend toward being "accused." This means you will need a very deep understanding of the grace of God. Everyone needs that understanding, but you will especially need to remember the words from Hebrews: "See to it that no one misses the grace of God" (12:15a), and the words spoken to Timothy (an "accused" fellow?): "You then, my son, be strong in the grace that is in Christ Jesus" (2 Timothy 2:1). The enemy knows he can get you feeling very discouraged over your weaknesses and your failures. He knows that the negative tapes begin to play and play loudly whenever you sin. You do not want to lose your sensitive conscience. You do not want to ever lose your ability to feel conviction, but when you sin, you need to focus on the fact that God forgives completely those with a broken and contrite heart. You will need to focus on passages like these:

This righteousness from God comes through faith in Jesus Christ to all who believe. There is no difference, for all have sinned and fall short of the glory of God, and are justified freely by his grace through the redemption that came by Christ Jesus (Romans 3:22-24).

What a wretched man I am! Who will rescue me from this body of death? Thanks be to God—through Jesus Christ our Lord!

So then, I myself in my mind am a slave to God's law, but in the sinful nature a slave to the law of sin.

Therefore, there is now no condemnation for those who are in Christ Jesus (Romans 7:24-8:1).

You probably need a printout of every passage that talks about grace. As an "accused" person you can become one who loves grace, rejoices in grace and celebrates grace. Such a focus will get you out of doubt and depression, out of the paralysis of analysis and out of self-pity.

If, on the other hand, you conclude that you have more tendencies toward being "excused," you will be served well by doing some serious study on humility. Your personality has many strengths (but I don't have to tell you that). But in order for God to use those strengths, you will need to come back often to passages such as these:

You save the humble
but bring low those whose eyes are haughty
(Psalm 18:27).

When pride comes, then comes disgrace,
but with humility comes wisdom (Proverbs 11:2).

Young men, in the same way be submissive to those who are older. All of you, clothe yourselves with humility toward one another, because,
> *"God opposes the proud*
>> *but gives grace to the humble" (1 Peter 5:5).*

And since your tendency is not to easily see your own sin, you will need to pray with sincerity this prayer of David:

Search me, O God, and know my heart;
>*test me and know my anxious thoughts.*
See if there is any offensive way in me,
>*and lead me in the way everlasting*
>*(Psalm 139:23-24).*

The more you pray like this, asking God to shine his spotlight on your sin so that you can see it clearly, the less the two-by-four will be needed! (That is good, because those things can hurt.)

This is a very brief letter about a very big subject, but I hope it helps you to think more about your tendencies and encourages you to talk this kind of thing over with others. The more you understand yourself, the more effective you will be in your struggle with the enemy.

14

Your Baptism

Dear new ones,

In this letter I am going to write to you about your baptism into Christ. This is a very biblical thing to do. When Peter and Paul wrote letters to young disciples, they frequently took them back to their baptisms and reminded them of all that happened at that point in their lives.

Baptism, sadly, is a controversial subject in the religious world. I say "sadly," because there was no controversy at all about it in the early church. One gets the idea that there was complete unity about its purpose and its meaning. Because it is controversial today, I am going to be extra careful in this chapter.

I am not worried about offending someone. I have counted the cost of including this section. I already know that this book would sell many more copies in religious bookstores if I would just leave out this chapter. No, it is not fear that motivates me. Instead, I am going to be very careful because I want it to be clear that everything I am saying here is connected directly to what the Bible says. I do not want anyone to be able to say that something was pulled out of context or distorted. I also want you to be able to share with others with the greatest of confidence what your baptism meant and what theirs can mean. I do not want you to ever feel apologetic for clear biblical teaching on this subject.

Christians baptize others who want to become disciples because Jesus commanded it. Once again we turn to Matthew 28:

> *Then Jesus came to them and said, "All authority in heaven and on earth has been given to me. Therefore go and make disciples of all nations, baptizing them in the name of the Father and of the Son and of the Holy Spirit, and teaching them to obey everything I have commanded you. And surely I am with you always, to the very end of the age" (Matthew 28:18-20).*

The mission is to go and teach people to become disciples. When people decide they want to accept that calling, they are to be baptized, and then they are to be discipled to Jesus—that is, taught to obey everything he commanded.

Some time ago, someone who was a disciple came into your life. In some way, that disciple asked if he or she could teach you what following Jesus is all about. After a short time or maybe a long time, you agreed. You heard Jesus' message and after some amount of time, you decided you needed him and his saving grace; and you said, "I want to be his disciple."

Immediately, arrangements were made for you to be baptized.

Peter's sermon in Acts 2 details for us what was being accomplished in your baptism. Speaking to the huge crowd gathered for the festival of Pentecost, Peter first told them about Jesus and how they had crucified him. Then we read these words:

> *When the people heard this, they were cut to the heart and said to Peter and the other apostles, "Brothers, what shall we do?"*
>
> *Peter replied, "Repent and be baptized, every one of you, in the name of Jesus Christ for the forgiveness of your sins. And you will receive the gift of the Holy Spirit"* *(Acts 2:37-38).*

Here we have an apostle of Christ, who had been given the keys to the kingdom of heaven (Matthew 16:19), on inauguration day for the church of Christ. He is telling the people who were cut to the heart what they must do and what would be done for them when they did it. He tells them to repent (to turn their minds and go in a new direction toward God) and to be baptized. He further explained what baptism accomplishes. He said it is "for the forgiveness of sins" and is followed by the gift of the Holy Spirit.

I probably do not need to say that all of this is very important. What can be more important than being forgiven of sin and receiving the gift of God's Spirit? Why would anyone want to teach anything different from what the leading apostle taught on the day when a whole new era began? Would God have allowed error in the definitive, for-all-time statement about how to become a Christian and how to become part of his church? Our all-powerful God had orchestrated this plan for centuries. Would he have blown it right when it was clearly culminating? I think we would all have to respond with a resounding "No!"

In response to God's clear message and direction through Peter, three thousand people were baptized that day in the area of the temple. (And as one who recently visited that spot, I can tell you that there were plenty of water pools there to accomplish that task.) But I want to remind you also that Peter promised that the same results of baptism in the name of Jesus would be for "all those that the Lord our God will call." That means you. That means a friend you are sharing with.

This same Peter and his fellow apostles then taught others this message, who passed it on to still others. Jesus' plan (in Matthew 28) began to work. One such person who learned this message was Philip, who became an evangelist. Through some Spirit-led decisions, he ended up sharing the good news with a man from Ethiopia. We could write much about this incident, but I include it here for one reason: We have been seeing what baptism is inwardly—a decision to repent and follow Jesus as Lord. But this passage makes it clear what baptism is outwardly:

> As they traveled along the road, they came to some water and the eunuch said, "Look, here is water. Why shouldn't I be baptized?" And he gave orders to stop the chariot. Then both Philip and the eunuch went down into the water and Philip baptized him (Acts 8:36-38).

I include this because some people today teach that baptism is only a spiritual experience, not a literal or a physical one. Obviously, this is not the case. We are talking here about immersion (from the Greek word *baptidzo* which means to "dip, plunge or immerse") in water. The picture is hard to misunderstand. Two grown men walked down into the water and one immersed the other. The one who was baptized then went on his way rejoicing (v. 39). He had found the Messiah. His sins had been forgiven. He had received the promised Holy Spirit. I trust that brings back memories for you.

So, first we have the command of Jesus, then we have the examples in the book of Acts (there are many more that we could look it), and now we come to the comments made to newer Christians in the letters of Paul and Peter.

First, we will look at Paul's statement in Romans 6. He has just been talking about how salvation is by grace, but he does not want anyone to think that grace means a license to sin. He says,

> *What shall we say, then? Shall we go on sinning so that grace may increase? By no means! We died to sin; how can we live in it any longer? Or don't you know that all of us who were baptized into Christ Jesus were baptized into his death? We were therefore buried with him through baptism into death in order that, just as Christ was raised from the dead through the glory of the Father, we too may live a new life (Romans 6:1-4).*

Paul's purpose was not to write a treatise on baptism. His purpose was to convince them that they should not continue in sin. To do this, he reminded them of their baptisms because what happened there needed to have a cataclysmic effect on sin in their lives. So what happens in baptism, according to Paul? (1) The disciple dies to sin. (2) The disciple is baptized into the death of Christ. (3) The disciple is buried with Christ through baptism. (4) The disciple is raised out of baptism to live a new life.

In the next two verses Paul added an exclamation mark to what he had already said:

> *If we have been united with him like this in his death, we will certainly also be united with him in his*

resurrection. For we know that our old self was crucified with him so that the body of sin might be done away with, that we should no longer be slaves to sin (Romans 6:5-6).

If we just read the text carefully, we see that baptism is a union with Christ—a union with his death, with his burial and with his resurrection. That union is said to bring us to new life. Your baptism was vital. It united you with Christ in whom you find saving grace and the power of the Holy Spirit. How can we who have experienced such a union ever go on willfully in sin? We have died and have risen with Christ.

Be thankful for what has happened to you. Make no apology about it. Preach it to others.

15

Is Doctrine Still Important?

Dear brothers and sisters,

Having just written you about baptism, I am thinking that it is a good time to write you about what is sometimes called "doctrine." In many churches today doctrine is one of those unfashionable words that many feel belong to a bygone era. Doctrine is viewed much like colonialism or segregation or apartheid—something widely accepted at one time, but no longer appropriate in a more enlightened age.

In their minds, to talk about doctrine is to sound narrow-minded and contentious. In our day the modern virtue is to accept each other using the lowest common denominator. It is not unusual to find churches that still claim to be Christian, yet completely accept (and make into leaders) those who do not believe in the authority of the Bible, the divinity of Christ or perhaps even in the existence of God.

Some churches believe that if you are seeking for something higher or nobler in life, if you have an appreciation for poetry or some of the deeper questions, then you are considered a fellow pilgrim and you are viewed as being as right as anyone else. You may find meaning in Christ or you may not. It does not really matter as long as you are committed to some notion of spirituality.

Those who still talk about doctrine are thought of as less enlightened, less sophisticated and certainly less cool. Since no one really wants to be thought of as "uncool," (the ultimate "sin" in our modern culture), there is tremendous pressure on Christians to compromise when it comes to doctrine.

As we know, culture is not our lord; Jesus is Lord. So what would Jesus have us do about doctrine? Doctrine is a very religious sounding word for a much more common word: teaching. *Doctrine is simply what you believe and what you teach others to believe.* Jesus was known as the Teacher. He taught the crowds. He taught his disciples. And, as we have seen, he taught them to go and teach others everything he had first taught them. There is no following of Jesus without believing certain truths and without holding on to those truths, while also teaching others to do the same. Listen to Jesus talking about his teaching (his doctrine):

> *To the Jews who had believed him, Jesus said, "If you hold to my teaching, you are really my disciples. Then you will know the truth, and the truth will set you free"* *(John 8:31-32).*

Teachings must not just be listened to; we must hold to them. His teachings are not just poetry to soothe the soul. His teachings are truth, and in holding tightly and consciously and carefully to his teachings, we are set free. Christianity is not a vague spiritual pilgrimage. It is a deliberate commitment to a body of teaching that leads to certain specific results. Never apologize for having clear beliefs and for teaching those to others.

Paul addressed this topic in his letters to Timothy and Titus. Here are several examples:

Watch your life and doctrine closely. Persevere in them, because if you do, you will save both yourself and your hearers (1 Timothy 4:16).

For the time will come when men will not put up with sound doctrine. Instead, to suit their own desires, they will gather around them a great number of teachers to say what their itching ears want to hear (2 Timothy 4:3).

He [an elder] must hold firmly to the trustworthy message as it has been taught, so that he can encourage others by sound doctrine and refute those who oppose it (Titus 1:9).

You must teach what is in accord with sound doctrine (Titus 2:1).

Doctrine is absolutely a concern. The phrase "sound doctrine" can more literally be translated "healthy teaching." Paul knows that what you teach matters. The right teaching leads to spiritual health. The wrong teaching leads to spiritual problems. Fashionable or not, doctrine still matters, and it will matter as long as the truth about God, Christ, the church and life matters.

In your life you will meet people who are spiritually minded. They will believe that there is something more than cars, houses, vacations and pleasure. They will talk about the need for spirituality. But you must still be concerned about what they believe about the Bible, about Jesus Christ, about the cross, about salvation, about the mission of a disciple. You must remember that it was Jesus who taught about the narrow door to life:

"Enter through the narrow gate. For wide is the gate and broad is the road that leads to destruction, and many enter through it. But small is the gate and narrow the road that leads to life, and only a few find it" (Matthew 7:13-14).

A lot of sophisticated people still pay lip service to Jesus, but with a message like this he would not be welcome at their dinner parties or their weekend conferences on spirituality. In our day, when broad-mindedness is considered the greatest virtue, Jesus himself would seem badly out of step. However, it is those who do not respect God's word and do not revere his teachings who are badly out of step.

Jesus spoke about false prophets who led people astray with their message (Matthew 7:16). He further taught that those who ignore God's message and who try their own form of spirituality are in for a rude awakening. He put it this way:

"Not everyone who says to me, 'Lord, Lord,' will enter the kingdom of heaven, but only he who does the will of my Father who is in heaven. Many will say to me on that day, 'Lord, Lord, did we not prophesy in your name, and in your name drive out demons and perform many miracles?' Then I will tell them plainly, 'I never knew you. Away from me, you evildoers!' " (Matthew 7:21-23).

That kind of message is not "politically correct" in these times. It probably is not one that members of your family would agree with, but it is a pointed reminder that God is concerned about what we teach and how we live. It is a reminder that other forms of spirituality are no substitute for the truth.

Just one word of caution: As you teach correct doctrine, do it gently and humbly. Take very seriously this word from Paul:

Don't have anything to do with foolish and stupid arguments, because you know they produce quarrels. And the Lord's servant must not quarrel; instead, he must be kind to everyone, able to teach, not resentful. Those who oppose him he must gently instruct, in the hope that God will grant them repentance leading them to a knowledge of the truth, and that they will come to their senses and escape from the trap of the devil, who has taken them captive to do his will (2 Timothy 2:23-26).

It is possible to have correct doctrine, and yet not be "right" because of a prideful, argumentative spirit. Decide today that you will hold on both to correct teaching and to a humble heart—they belong together.

16
Living with
Joy and Gratitude

Dear disciples,

Each of you reading this book is at a different point in your journey. Some of you may be in your first month. Others of you may be approaching six months or even a year as a disciple. A few old-timers, who have been around for years, may be secretly reading some of these letters after everyone else has gone to bed. Regardless of your time in the kingdom, I suspect you already realize that a lot of tough things happen to disciples. I am going to talk about some more of these before this book is done. However, I want to let you know in this letter that no matter how many tough things happen, you always have a reason to be grateful, and you always have a reason to be joyful. I think I can convince you that this is true.

God has blessed us. He has not given us a perfect life, but in this life he has given us many blessings. I have multiple sclerosis. It is often described in medical literature as a horrible disease. Many sufferers feel it has ruined their lives. I certainly find it challenging, but I don't in any way feel my life is horrible. I have so many other blessings. At the head of the list, I have a friendship with God, made possible by the death and resurrection of Jesus Christ. As I wrote you earlier, I can walk with him and talk with him and get direction, comfort and support from him. I join with David in saying to God, "Because your love is better than life, my lips will glorify you" (Psalm 63:3). If I had no other good thing in my life except a walk with God, I would still have enough to give me joy.

I don't know what your challenges are, but I know we all have them. You may have a spouse who is not a disciple, or you may have a chronic illness or a disability. You may have come into the kingdom with a truckload of financial or family problems that are going to take time to resolve. You may have been a "user" and now you are going to have to work hard to stay clean. But whatever your trials, you have the same great blessing that I have. You have a friendship with the Lord of the Cosmos, the King of the Universe, the Everlasting Father and the Wonderful Counselor. You have the best reason in the world to stay thankful and to stay joyful.

Some time ago I came across a passage from Nehemiah 8:10. (I think this is the first time I have mentioned him, but his book is a great one!) Here is what it says:

Nehemiah said, "Go and enjoy choice food and sweet drinks, and send some to those who have nothing prepared. This day is sacred to our Lord. Do not grieve, for the joy of the LORD is your strength" (Nehemiah 8:10).

It was that last phrase that caught my attention: *the joy of the Lord is my strength.* As I meditated on that idea, it occurred me that there is (1) the joy that comes from *who God is,* (2) the joy that comes from *what God has done,* (3) the joy that comes from *what God is doing* and (4) the joy that comes from *what God has promised to do.*

Who God is, is enough to produce gratitude. He is not a cosmic tyrant but a Heavenly Father who loves us with all the best qualities of a great father and great mother (Matthew 7:11, Psalm 131:2, Isaiah 66:13).

What God has done is enough to bring joy. He gave the best he had to give to atone for my sins. I am standing before him without blemish and free from accusation because he sent his Son to be the atoning sacrifice for my sins (Colossians 1:22). Two nights ago, a disciple in her thirties died in her sleep. It was totally unexpected. We were shocked, but as a disciple, she died completely forgiven and pure before God. Disciples at her memorial service will weep, but through the tears we will see the joy set before her. Something God did in the past gives me and every disciple tremendous reason for joy and thanksgiving.

What God is doing right now is enough to bring joy. We have already pointed out that God is always at work (John 5:17). We have also pointed out that he is always working for the good of those who love him (Romans 8:28). For what more can I ask? If you knew one of the world's most powerful and influential people was working every day for your good, I know it would encourage you. If you knew he was on the phone calling other important people in your behalf, if you knew he was telling his financial officer to spend whatever was needed to help you, and if you knew he was ready to make his many homes and his personal jet available to you, you would feel pretty important and pretty good about life. You might have a disease or another serious problem, but you would rejoice that you had this much support. But as a disciple, you have more. You have the God of this universe working every day for your good. If that doesn't cause us to rejoice, what will?

Finally, what God has promised to do is enough to bring joy. What he has promised, of course, is to give us abundant life with him forever. I mentioned earlier that many of these letters are being written from a cabin in New Hampshire. I don't come here often. The last time was three years ago, but it is a great place to write. At this very moment, as I write these words, I am sitting on a screened-in porch. A gentle fall breeze is blowing, and the trees are making their own melody. The temperature is near perfect. A beautiful lake-size pond spreads out before me, the water sparkling and lapping softly against the shore. I almost want to ask: "Is this heaven?" The answer, of course, would be, "No, this is New Hampshire" (for those of you who have seen *Field of Dreams*). The truth is, as beautiful as this is and as much as it restores my soul to be here, this is nothing compared to what God is going to give us some day. Every battle in the Christian life will be worth it. Every late night working to bring in another soul will be worth it. Every time of wearing our bodies out in serving others will be worth it. Every insult endured will be worth it.

So here is the message: Whatever happens, don't lose your joy. You have good reason to keep it. You will have to remind yourself of this on certain days. You may have to reread this letter a few times. But let joy and gratitude fill your life. God is enough.

From now until your life ends, you will face things that will be difficult. You will have a "bad" day or a "bad" week. But nothing that happens will change God's eternal nature, his tireless work and his unconditional love for you. You will always have good reasons to "rejoice in the Lord" (Philippians 4:4). You have a source of joy that the world knows nothing about. Turn the handle, and let it flow.

17
Hitting the Lows

Dear friends,

Almost all Christians go through times when their spirits dip. Sometimes we get *discouraged*. Things we thought would happen don't. Efforts we made don't bring the results we thought were promised. We invest a lot and seem to get little in return. Or maybe a relationship just does not seem to be working out. Perhaps the person discipling us does not seem to understand us, or we do not relate well with him or her. "Best Friends for All Time" was the title of one of the follow-up studies done with us after baptism, but we don't see how this relationship is going to become a best-friend type of relationship.

Sometimes we get *confused*. We are not sure how some things in the Bible fit together. Or we meet some very nice and sincere people who don't really follow the Bible. They are wrong, but their lives seem to be working out very well. There seems to be a conflict between our experience and what we have been taught. Or maybe some family members really start putting on the pressure. Maybe they are hurt that we no longer seem to consider their spiritual experience to be the same as ours, and their comments tend to reflect more and more bitterness. Maybe our faith and convictions seem to be driving a wedge between us and loved ones.

And then some of us start having *doubts*. Perhaps we start to doubt the necessity of some things we have been taught, or maybe something happens that causes us to doubt God himself. We wonder if we should even be in the church with these doubts. We wonder if our doubts won't pull others down. We reason that it would be better for everyone if we just were not around.

The worst mistake we make in any of these times is to think that we are unusual. We look around and no one else *seems* to be having these struggles. But the truth is that the great majority of disciples go through such times, and you need to know two things. (1) It is okay to struggle. You are not weird. Nothing strange is happening. (2) You will be fine if you get a grip on a big word in the Bible: perseverance.

You have made the right decision. You are on a road that brings life now and life forever. You are living with a purpose, and you are making a difference in the world. You are part of a giant worldwide family that is taking the message of Jesus to the ends of the earth. As you go about all this, you hit some lows because there is an enemy who does not want you to continue. He pours on the unholy trio: discouragement, confusion and doubt. But you are not the first person he has hit with these things, and there are plenty of examples around you of those who have been hit and hit again, but who have persevered.

Perseverance is a big word for a very simple idea—*never quit*. When you signed up to be a disciple of Jesus, it was like getting married. You made a commitment to someone and to his cause. You essentially said, "Wherever you go, I will go; your people will be my people. I will be faithful to you until death." Take it from someone married almost thirty years: One of the most crucial ingredients in a long-lasting and happy marriage is the attitude that says *I will never quit*. And that is the same attitude that must be there in our relationship with Christ. Just as we hit lows in marriage, we hit them in our relationship with Christ and his church. But we must never quit, and the Bible says—and my experience says—we will be rewarded. The long term effects of perseverance are incredible!

We live in times when people are soft and weak in character. They try something until it gets hard. Then they quit and try something else. We must be different. Listen to a few passages about how tough times will come and how God uses those times when we practice perseverance:

> Not only so, but we also rejoice in our sufferings, because we know that suffering produces perseverance; perseverance, character; and character, hope (Romans 5:3-4).

> Remember those earlier days after you had received the light, when you stood your ground in a great contest in the face of suffering....So do not throw away your confidence; it will be richly rewarded. You need to persevere so that when you have done the will of God, you will receive what he has promised (Hebrews 10:32, 35-36).

...because you know that the testing of your faith develops perseverance. Perseverance must finish its work so that you may be mature and complete, not lacking anything (James 1:3-4).

Certainly you have noticed that when a sports team sets itself as a real contender, it is not long before another team comes along to test them. You know more about what they are made of after the test has come. It is easy to talk the talk, but, as they say, can you walk the walk?

After we make a commitment to follow Jesus as Lord, the tests will follow. Tests, by their very nature, are hard. Tests, by their very nature, cause many to consider quitting. But do you hear what the Scriptures are saying? They are saying that the tests, the suffering, the difficulties and the trials can all serve a very good purpose. As we develop perseverance and move on through those times of testing, we develop deeper character and greater spiritual maturity.

And so I say to you, don't think you are an oddball when you find yourself struggling. Don't let appearances fool you. Other disciples struggle. Don't think, *I don't belong here.* You are not alone. But I also say to you, don't be a child of this age. Don't think, like so many today, that you can always quit if the going gets tough. Take to heart these words spoken to struggling disciples more than 1900 years ago:

Therefore, since we are surrounded by such a great cloud of witnesses, let us throw off everything that hinders and the sin that so easily entangles, and let us run with perseverance the race marked out for us (Hebrews 12:1).

The "great cloud of witnesses" he refers to are all those heroes of the faith he has just mentioned in Hebrews 11. It is as though all those great people from the Old Testament are sitting in the arena cheering for us. Encouraged by that thought, the writer tells us to take all the needed steps to run with perseverance—with dogged determination. And then he adds:

> *Let us fix our eyes on Jesus, the author and perfecter of our faith, who for the joy set before him endured the cross, scorning its shame, and sat down at the right hand of the throne of God. Consider him who endured such opposition from sinful men, so that you will not grow weary and lose heart (Hebrews 12:2-3).*

If you need an example of perseverance, you need look no further than Jesus. At some point, you will be severely tested. It may seem that all the demons of hell have been marshaled to try to pull you out of the kingdom. It may seem the enemy is employing a full-court press. But, like great heroes of the faith who have gone before you, you can make it. You can fix your eyes on Jesus and say, "I will never quit." The man or woman who emerges on the other side of those trials and battles will be a wiser and spiritually richer person.

Never quit.

18
Opposition and Persecution

My fellow disciples,

I am very thankful to be a Christian. I love being a disciple. When all things are considered, I know it just doesn't get any better than this. But there are still unpleasant things to be faced, and right at the top of that list is persecution. What an ugly word. Just the sound of it makes you shudder. I have seen in Christians' lives that very often nothing is more unsettling than persecution. No one likes it. No one wants it. Some are shaken terribly by it. However, persecution is a fact of life for disciples of Jesus.

Some people think that the presence of persecution indicates you did something wrong. I remember some church leaders in a denominational setting many years ago telling me, "We have been in this town and on this university campus for forty years. We have never been persecuted, and we do not want it to start now." That was their way of rebuking me for some trouble we had stirred up by preaching Jesus' radical message of commitment. They were telling me to tone down my message because it was resulting in too much reaction.

Their challenge sent me back to my Bible where I found that persecution is predicted, expected and normal in the lives of those who follow Jesus of Nazareth. Listen to these words of Jesus which are typical in the New Testament:

"If the world hates you, keep in mind that it hated me first. If you belonged to the world, it would love you as its own. As it is, you do not belong to the world, but I have chosen you out of the world. That is why the world hates you. Remember the words I spoke to you: 'No servant is greater than his master.' If they persecuted me, they will persecute you also. If they obeyed my teaching, they will obey yours also. They will treat you this way because of my name, for they do not know the One who sent me " (John 15:18-21).

Consider this: Suppose an American who is a real patriot moves to one of the countries in the world that is still communist. Just pick one. Suppose he moves into an apartment and hangs his American flag out the window. Suppose he opens his window and plays "The Star Spangled Banner" so that the strains are heard down the block. Suppose he goes on the street selling tapes touting the value of the free enterprise system and showing how socialism strangles the economy and the spirit of the people. (Please understand—I am not advocating this course of action. I am just using it as an illustration.) Now, what sort of reaction is he going to get? He is living under one system, but he is very much acting like he is a citizen of another country with a totally different system. That will get him in trouble.

That, very simply, my friends, is why Christians get in trouble; and that is why persecution comes. We live in this world (where there is a certain system), and yet we are citizens of heaven (Philippians 3:20) and live by a totally different system. It is the right way to live. It is of God. But the world does not like it. It is offensive to those who have no desire to please God. That is essentially what Jesus says in John 15:19, "You do not belong to the world, and that is why they hate you." You don't live by their system anymore.

No one likes persecution, and in the church we are always thinking about every godly thing we can do to reduce occurrences. But we will never—in this world—stop persecution. The only way we can do that is to do what those leaders wanted me to do years ago—tone down the message of Jesus, and that is just not an option for us (although many churches have chosen that more popular route).

Persecution can take various forms. Exact definitions are hard to come by, but in my mind, there is criticism and opposition, and then there is serious persecution (which may involve physical abuse, legal action or disowning). I have experienced a good deal of the criticism and opposition. I hear stories about brothers and sisters who have experienced the latter.

Fifteen times the New Testament uses the words "oppose" or "opposition" to describe a reaction that came to the message of Jesus or the work of the ministry. There is nothing surprising here. There is opposition to everything. A man in the town where I live wanted to open an ice cream stand, and there was enormous opposition to it. I just heard on the radio about another businessman who wants to enlarge his egg farm in Vermont, but the citizens of the nearby town are out in front of his property protesting and opposing his expansion. Opposition is everywhere. Christians are opposed. So what? Why would that be surprising?

In our day opposition (usually on the part of religious leaders) to the work of disciples often leads to stories in the media. Here it is not uncommon to find all kinds of distortions, half-truths and slanderous accusations being made. Television and newspaper executives in these times have learned that only the sensational sells, and there are always plenty of critics of the church around who are glad to cooperate in making the work of the church sound like something horrible. (What else is new? The critics of the early Christians called them cannibals and atheists.)

But here is the challenge. We live in such a media-oriented age. Most people don't trust the media to tell the truth about them, and yet they eat up what it has to say about others. And so when some big stories run in the papers, magazines or on the television describing the church as a dangerous cult, we feel really injured. In reality nothing that serious has happened. Our property has not been confiscated. No crosses have been burned on our front lawns. We have not been beaten. Our children have not been taken from us. But we feel abused. We feel embarrassed that our church has received so much negative publicity. Sometimes young Christians let all this really shake them.

It is understandable. But right here is where you need to hear some words written by Peter to others going through similar opposition:

> *Dear friends, do not be surprised at the painful trial you are suffering, as though something strange were happening to you. But rejoice that you participate in the sufferings of Christ, so that you may be overjoyed when his glory is revealed. If you are insulted because of the name of Christ, you are blessed, for the Spirit of glory and of God rests on you (1 Peter 4:12-14).*

"Do not be surprised." The first time you read an article that alleges that leaders you know are dangerous and that the practice of discipling one another is the same as mind control, let's be honest, it does surprise you. In fact, it probably shocks you. And it may even shake you in a big way. Peter was trying to prepare his new friends in the faith for this. The world will always react to true discipleship. That reaction may surprise us but Scripture tells us it is to be expected.

I believe that we can learn things from our critics. Sometimes they have a point worth considering, but we can never make enough changes—and still be faithful to the Bible—to ever please or stop the critics. So when the slanderous accusations come, talk it over with others, get advice about how to respond, and go back and look at the many references in the New Testament to opposition and persecution. Remind yourself that nothing strange is happening. Pray for courage, and remember these words from the writer of Hebrews:

> *Consider him [Jesus] who endured such opposition from sinful men, so that you will not grow weary and lose heart (Hebrews 12:3).*

19
Remember the Poor

Dear fellow Christians,

A few days or a few weeks ago when you decided to follow Jesus Christ and be an imitator of his lifestyle, you made a commitment to love the poor, because Jesus loved the poor. For some of you this will represent a major change. Many people in first-world countries become disciples having never been involved with the poor and the needy. It will mean stepping out of your comfort zone. It will mean going to places you may seldom go. But careful study of the Bible reveals that God has always had a heart for the poor and that he has always called his people to get involved in their lives.

In Matthew 25 Jesus tells the parable of the sheep and the goats. Stop now and read what he says in verses 31-46. In the context of all Jesus' teachings and those found in the rest of the New Testament, it would be a mistake to think that Jesus is saying that all those who feed the poor will be saved and those who do not will be lost. Our salvation is not by works, but by grace. However, he certainly is making the point that those who really have a relationship with God will be people who care for those in need and that you could not possibly have a saving relationship with God if you remain indifferent to those who are poor and needy.

If you are like some of the rest of us, you may look at these teachings and say, "But where do I start?" Some of us are surrounded by people who may be spiritually impoverished, but when it comes to physical things, they are doing fine. In recent years those of us in discipling and restoring churches have done a great deal of thinking about these matters in an effort to identify needs and find ways to serve. If you will ask for help, you will surely find people in your ministry who can help channel you in the right direction.

One of the groups you will hear about is HOPE *worldwide*. This organization, while separate from the church, was started a number of years ago by concerned disciples who wanted to increase our effectiveness in working with the poor. HOPE has many programs that offer disciples and others opportunities to get involved both locally and in far-flung places around the world. Thousands of disciples participate each year in the HOPE for Kids effort which sends them into cities to find parents whose children need immunizations and to provide them with information about how to get these important shots for their kids. Many churches have special efforts to provide foster care, assist in adoptions, provide toys at Christmas, reach out to orphanages, visit nursing homes, help the homeless and meet many other needs.

As I write this, friends of ours are far from those of us here in the US. Dr. Graham Gumley is a noted hand surgeon with a practice at a major medical facility in the Boston area. Some time ago, he and his wife, Suzanne, made the decision to take their three young children and move to Phnom Phen, Cambodia, for a year. They went so that Graham could become a staff member at the Sihanouk Center of HOPE hospital—a hospital completely directed by HOPE *worldwide*. There in Phnom Phen they joined another couple from our Boston congregation— Cam and Shiara Gifford, who had left for Cambodia six months earlier. There Graham is able to use his skills to particularly help those who had been maimed by some of the thousands of land mines found in that country.

As they prepared for the move, civil war broke out in Cambodia. The Gumleys waited until the dust had settled and some semblance of order was replaced, and then they moved forward with their plans. They are making a major sacrifice. They have taken their children into a situation that is unstable. Why? Because they have committed themselves to love the poor and to be open to how God wants to use them to help. You can be sure that God is well pleased with such decisions.

I do not know how God will use you, but I know that you have something to give, and I know that as you give it, you will be following in the steps of Jesus. Caring for the poor must never replace going and making disciples as the mission of the church—but it does not have to. The two go hand in hand. As we reach out to the poor, we let our lights shine. We show the world that we care, and that caring opens all kinds of doors to reach out spiritually. We will have opportunities to bring the poor to Christ, and he is the one they need the most. We will also make an impression on people in the community and have a greater opportunity to share our spiritual convictions with them.

As you think about loving the poor, answer a few questions. (1) How has God blessed you financially? (2) Do you have extra that could be used to relieve needs that others have? (3) What skills do you have that could be used in programs to help the poor? (I know people using their knowledge of computers, their skills in carpentry, their ability to organize people, their love for children—all to help the poor.) (4) Who in your congregation is a key person in the work of HOPE *worldwide* or some other, similar effort? Have you had any discussions with them about their work and asked how you can help? (5) How much time are you willing to sacrifice to help the poor?

The book of Proverbs is full of counsel about caring for the poor. I close this letter with two verses for you to ponder:

> *He who gives to the poor will lack nothing,*
> *but he who closes his eyes to them receives many*
> *curses (Proverbs 28:27).*

> *The righteous care about justice for the poor,*
> *but the wicked have no such concern (Proverbs*
> *29:7).*

As you follow Jesus, remember the poor, love the poor, give time, money and care to the poor, and you will be blessed.

20

When the World Looks Good

Dear brothers and sisters,

I love the kingdom of God. I think being a disciple is the very best way to live. And, yet, if I am honest with you, I will admit that there are times when the world (meaning the non-Christian life-style), or at least, something it has to offer, looks good. I know if that happens to a grisly old Christian like me, I am quite sure that it will happen to you. When we become disciples, we see through a lot of the world's appeal, but there are times when something about the world looks attractive to us all.

We have already looked at the enemy and at the fact that he tailor-makes his schemes for each one of us. This means that the appeal of the world is going to come to us in different ways. Something that is attractive to me may not bother you at all and vice versa.

But from time to time, *something* will come along outside of Christ and outside of the discipline and rigors of commitment that looks very appealing to us all. For most of you there was something that brought you comfort or pleasure before you became a Christian. When the heat gets turned up on your discipleship, some of those things may suddenly seem very appealing again.

I have told you earlier that most of these letters were written while my wife and I stayed in a cabin in New Hampshire. We are back home now as I write some of the final letters, but I must tell you, that life there—far away from the phone, the distractions and the disruptions—began to look very good. I found it a bit hard to pack the bags after just four days in that beautiful and somewhat isolated spot and start back for the Boston suburbs, knowing that needs and problems in other people's lives awaited us there, as they always do. Across the way from us, I could see another property where the owner of a nice, year-round home had a canoe, a sailboat and a ski boat. It all looked pretty good.

When I told my friend Gordon Ferguson (if you haven't seen some of his books, you probably will) about this, his comment was an interesting one: "Oh, I know. If I were not a disciple, I would definitely live some place like that, far away from most human inhabitation." Now, you may not be tempted at all by the things that tempt older guys like us. You may be the kind of person who goes nuts if you aren't right in the middle of one of the world's great urban areas, but this I know: *There is something about the world that will at some time start looking good to you.*

It can seem sometimes that our commitment to Jesus is interfering with "the good life." If I was not spending so much time reaching out to others and attending so many meetings, I would have more time to do X, Y and Z. If was not giving so much money to the kingdom, I would have enough left over to buy this and that. Joe Christian walks out of his house on a Sunday morning, through his yard he just could not find the time to work on, and gets into his seven-year-old Toyota. He sees across the street his neighbor's shiny new car (you pick a brand), observes his well manicured lawn, and looks a bit enviously at him coming out in his shorts to get the morning paper—the first act in a day of sheer relaxation. Or Sally Christian leaves her apartment in downtown Metropolis and sees her neighbor lacing up the roller blades for a day of cruising through the park. We cannot deny it. There are moments when the world looks pretty good.

The attraction of the world is especially powerful when you personally are being opposed for your faith or when the church is undergoing some persecution in the community. The world also starts looking better and better when you are going through some struggle to change your character, and there are disciples in your life bringing you some strong but needed challenges. Such change means hard work. From somewhere you hear a voice saying, "There is a much more comfortable life you could be living."

The truth is, there is a more *comfortable* life you could be living, but there are things more important than comfort. The writer of Psalm 73 fully experienced what I am describing in this letter. Before you read on, take your Bible and read what he wrote.

You can see that he looked at his unspiritual neighbors and wondered out loud if they did not have it better than he did. "In vain I have kept my heart pure," he moans. In other words, "I have worked hard at being what God wants me to be, and it looks like other people who don't care about God have it better than I do." But then he did what we need to do. He went to worship (verse 17) and something happened in that experience that reminded him of "the final destiny" of those who do not seek or love God. There are snapshots of the lives of non-Christians that look good. Here they are roller-blading carefreely on a Sunday morning. Here they are in their sailboat. Here they are taking off on another weekend trip in their new, sport-utility vehicle! But those snapshots do not represent the whole picture.

First, there are all kinds of things going on behind the scenes. If non-Christians have it so great, why do so many of their marriages end in messy divorces? Why are so many of their kids doing drugs? Why are so many singles running ads in the paper that read "Attractive SWF looking for male companionship"? Do not be faked out by outward appearances. "The good life" may be only skin deep. When you probe a bit, you find it often isn't so great. (Surely some of us can remember this.) But then, there is the issue that the writer of our psalm brings up: their final destiny. Even if life in this world were better for the non-Christians (which it is not), there would still be the issue of final destiny. And "final" destinies are for eternity.

There will be times when the world looks good to us all. There will be times when it seems life might just be better if we let go of all this radical commitment to Jesus. At such times, let me urge you to come back to Psalm 73. Let me also urge you to sit down and make a list of all the blessings you have in Christ that you would lose if you left him. The truth is, whatever you give up to follow Jesus, you can afford to give up. What you get by being his disciple, you cannot afford to lose.

Do not love the world or anything in the world. If anyone loves the world—the love of the Father is not in him. For everything in the world—the cravings of sinful man, the lust of his eyes and the boasting of what he has and does—comes not from the Father but from the world. The world and its desires pass away, but the man who does the will of God lives forever (1 John 2:15-17).

21
Time and Money

Dear brothers and sisters,

When you made the decision that Jesus would be Lord of your life, you decided to put everything under his control. Jesus told a crowd of potential followers: "In the same way, any of you who does not give up everything he has cannot be my disciple" (Luke 14:33). Don't ever forget this verse. If you are ever tempted to think that the church calls for too much commitment, remember this verse. Remember that these are the words of Jesus. Discipleship involves *everything*.

He asks for everything for at least two reasons. (1) It is all his anyway, and disciples are people who have come to recognize this. (2) Once it is surrendered to him, he is able to make so much more from it than we are. A disciple then, is one who says to Jesus, "Here is my life—all of it. Take it and use it any way you see fit. Take me anywhere and do anything with me that pleases you."

When we surrender everything to Jesus, it means a whole new way of looking at two big issues in our lives: time and money. We must no longer think of these things as ours to spend or to waste in any way we choose. No, these are both now to be placed under the lordship and control of Jesus. Time and money are to be spent in ways that bring honor to him and in ways that advance his kingdom.

Now, before you sell everything you have and give the money to the church, and before you quit your job so you can spend all of your time out making disciples and doing other godly works, let's think for a minute about those decisions. In the overwhelming majority of cases, that is not what God has in mind for us. First, as we read through the New Testament and see the life of the early church under the direction of Jesus' apostles, we see that most Christians did not quit their jobs, and most of them did not sell everything that they had. On the contrary, even a leader like Paul worked as a tent-maker, and he exhorted others to settle down and earn a living (2 Thessalonians 3:12). Second, we know that if everyone in the church were to give up working, the kingdom would stop in its tracks because there would be no way to financially support the effort.

So, what is the answer? What steps do we take to put our time and money under the lordship of Jesus? First, we must take stock of the essentials that must be in every disciple's life. Consider these:

- Relationship with God (Mark 1:35, John 17:3)
- Relationships with family (Ephesians 5:22-6:4)
- Responsibility to work (1 Corinthians 4:12, Ephesians 4:28, 2 Thessalonians 3:12)
- Relationships with Christians (Romans 12:10, Hebrews 3:12)
- Relationships with the lost (Matthew 28:18-20)
- Rest and relaxation (Genesis 2:2, Exodus 16:30)

Since every one of these is called for (or inferred) in the Scriptures, we must plan our time so that not one of these is omitted. We must find the places where time is being wasted, thus keeping us from fulfilling God's plans. This requires fore-thought and is greatly facilitated by advice from those who have been working with such issues for a long time. With good counsel we can see how to combine different activities to ac-complish several goals at once. We can evaluate if we need to ask for a change in our work situation or look for another job that fits better with spiritual priorities.

When it comes to our use of money, we can see from Scripture other definite expectations that God has:

- Support of our families (1 Timothy 5:8)
- Support of the gospel (2 Corinthians 11:7-8, Philippians 4:15-16)
- Giving to the poor (Galatians 2:10)
- Showing hospitality (Romans 12:13, 1 Peter 4:9)
- Helping disciples and others in need (Galatians 6:10, Ephesians 4:28)

Putting our money under the lordship of Jesus means getting our financial houses in order so that we neglect none of these areas and can give generously to causes that build up the kingdom (2 Corinthians 9:6). Because we live in a world of easy credit and undisciplined spending, the first things many of us have to do as new disciples are to simplify our life-styles and to develop plans to get out of debt. We may also need to evaluate our job situations to see if we are underemployed. While doing all of this, we must take heed to the warnings given about money, such as this one that Paul delivered in 1 Timothy 6:

But godliness with contentment is great gain. For we brought nothing into the world, and we can take nothing out of it. But if we have food and clothing, we will be content with that. People who want to get rich fall into temptation and a trap *and into many foolish and harmful desires that plunge men into ruin and destruction.* For the love of money is a root of all kinds of evil. *Some people, eager for money, have wandered from the faith and pierced themselves with many griefs (1 Timothy 6:6-10, emphasis added).*

A luxurious and extravagant life-style does not fit with the priorities of discipleship. Having every new gadget and every fashionable item of clothing that is unveiled cannot be your goal. When it comes to money and the things it can buy, contentment is the key word. We are foolish if we forget that the pursuit of money and things is a trap where many have lost their souls.

God has blessed us all with the same amount of time. Surrendering it all to Jesus will not mean a constant state of exhaustion, but a state of fulfillment and a sense of deep accomplishment. When it comes to money, disciples find themselves at many different income levels. But each of us, from the richest to the poorest, must surrender our situations to God, develop contentment in our hearts and learn that God loves a cheerful giver. When your time and your money are in God's hands, the result will be a stronger church and a happier you.

22
The Power
and Satisfaction
of Serving

Dear fellow disciples,

My guess is that before you became a Christian, the whole idea of being a servant was not a very appealing one. We know for sure that it was not a thrilling idea to Jesus' first group of disciples. They were interested in positions of influence, not in opportunities to be servants (Mark 10:35-37). But Jesus seized the moment when they requested power and used it as a time to redefine greatness:

Jesus called them together and said, "You know that those who are regarded as rulers of the Gentiles lord it over them, and their high officials exercise authority over them. Not so with you. Instead, whoever wants to become great among you must be your servant, and whoever wants to be first must be slave of all. For even the Son of Man did not come to be served, but to serve, and to give his life as a ransom for many" (Mark 10:42-45).

Do you hear what he is saying? Being a servant is at the very heart of Jesus' life. Here is the man who knows more about how to live than anyone, and he says the one who is great is the one who is the servant—even the slave—of all. He was the divine Son of Man, but he says "Even I did not come to be served but to serve." Indeed, following this Jesus means a radical realignment of your thinking.

Let me test you. How do you feel about serving? When you are asked to help with a move, with a project for the poor, or with a dinner or a service for the church, are you eager to respond? In most of our churches there is a tremendous need for people to serve with the children's ministry. Are you ready and willing? Do others say about you: "S/he loves to serve"? What is your reputation when it comes to serving? Do you see your attitudes changing? Are you starting to enjoy serving?

It is okay if you do not yet pass the test with flying colors, as long as you want to learn. Most of us do not enter the kingdom with all the right attitudes on this point. We need to let Jesus teach us the power and the satisfaction of serving, as he taught the Twelve.

Let me talk about *the power of serving*. Serving does not look powerful to most people. That is part of the reason they aren't interested in it. But from Scripture we learn that the most powerful event in human history was an act of service—an unbelievably humble and costly act of service. Paul tells us that even though Jesus was in his very nature God, he became in his very nature a servant, and that as a servant he became obedient to death—even death on a cross (see Philippians 2:5-8). At the cross Jesus was certainly not serving himself but all of us. No event has changed more lives than that act of service. Here we come to the real definition of power. Something is powerful in God's eyes if it helps people, if it changes lives, if it gives people a clearer picture of him, if it draws people to him, if it causes people to have new hearts and new minds.

Whenever we serve happily in the name of Christ, we do something powerful. We *show* the world and our fellow disciples the message of Jesus. When we serve, we are not just talking the walk. We are walking the talk. We are giving people a vivid picture of Jesus' teaching. Speaking of the time Jesus washed his disciples' feet, John said,

> *Having loved his own who were in the world, he now showed them the full extent of his love (John 13:1).*

When you serve people, you *show them your love*, and when people feel loved, something great has happened (1 Corinthians 13:13).

Whenever people visit a church and they sense that people are not eager to serve, it is most unlikely that they will ever come back—no matter how correct the teaching in that church might be. But when they see people serving willingly and with enthusiasm, they are moved. Their hearts are touched. Something inside tells them that this is right and good. Many have opened their lives to the gospel just because of the way they have seen Christians serving. When you do something that opens someone's life to the gospel, be it at church, in your neighborhood, in your community or on a dormitory hall, you have done something powerful.

But let me talk also about *the satisfaction of serving*. There are two basic ways to live your life. You can seek to *get* or you can seek to *give*. Most of the world is concerned about getting. Jesus told us to concentrate on giving. Most of us have been taught by the world that you find your life by grabbing all you can and then holding on to it. But how many people with this philosophy seem very satisfied? Jesus brought us a message that says, "Whoever loses his life for me will find it" (Matthew 16:25). He taught that you find life by losing it. But what does he mean by "find it"? This is not the whole answer, but I am convinced he means you will find satisfaction.

There is something intensely satisfying about doing something for others. Jesus said it: "It is more blessed to give than to receive" (Acts 20:35). When you give your time, your energy, your money to help others, you end up feeling blessed by God. Just as your visitor to church knows he has seen something good when he sees disciples serving, you know instinctively that you have done the right thing when you help to meet a need. Something inside just feels very right about it.

Since the greatest servant of all was Jesus, you will never outgrow your need to be a servant. As you mature as disciples, some of you will be asked to take on different responsibilities of leadership. But no matter what position you are in, you must never forget Jesus' words: "Whoever wants to become great among you must be your servant, and whoever wants to be first must be slave of all" (Mark 10:43—44). How will you serve this week?

23
At the foot of the Cross

Dear brothers and sisters,

As I am nearing the completion of this book, I am thinking about how my time with you is almost up. In this letter and the one that follows, I want to give you two things to hold on to that are vital for all disciples. One of these, which I will talk with you about in this letter, is to always stay at the foot of the cross.

Before Jesus came, a cross would never have appeared in any spiritual book. No one would have even remotely connected a cross with a relationship with God. Crosses were despised and reviled. Slaves, insurrectionists and the worst of criminals died on crosses. But God does not work according to man's formulas and preconceived ideas. Several years ago I wrote this at the beginning of the book, *Thirty Days at the Foot of the Cross*:

Paul the Apostle said it as well as it can be said. He understood it as well as it can be understood. He hit the nail on the head. *"The message of the cross is foolishness to those who are perishing, but to us who are being saved it is the power of God"* (1 Corinthians 1:18). Twenty centuries ago the God of the universe made a surprise attack on the forces of darkness. He did what hardly anyone was expecting. He came as a baby and died on a cross. We are badly mistaken if we think that was easy for first century people to believe, but hard for people today. It was hard to believe then. It was hard for those closest to Jesus to believe. To many people it was downright foolishness. But to those who believed, to those who looked closely and decided there is good reason to believe, it was nothing less than the most powerful revelation ever received from the living God.

Nothing tells us more about life than this death. No event shows us more the character of God. No speech ever spoke so clearly about the values we all need. What happened when Jesus of Nazareth went to that hill outside the city gates will never in this world be fully understood. No scholar, preacher or poet can really take us to its depths. No one can fully fathom the mysteries that are here, but the closer we can get to it all, the better we will be. God wants a mighty movement in our day that will advance against darkness on every continent. But he will bless no movement that is not centered on the cross of Jesus Christ.[*]

Now, four years later, there is still nothing I believe more deeply. It is at the cross that we learn the most about God and the most about the attitudes that we need to have. I stand in awe of how many different needs in my life are met at the cross.

[*] Jones, Thomas and Sheila, editors, *Thirty Days at the Foot of the Cross* (Woburn, Mass.: Discipleship Publications International, 1994) p. 10.

When I am feeling lousy about myself and am wondering if God could possibly forgive me again, I come back to the cross and realize that he can. When I get proud, thinking that somehow I have done something really impressive, I come back to the cross and see what it took to redeem a sinner such as I. When I am having difficulty forgiving someone, I come back to the cross and remember the many times I've been forgiven. I remember that I am to forgive just as God, in Christ, forgave me.

When I am feeling selfish and am tired of giving, I come to the foot of the cross to understand again just how far love must go. When I am in a conflict with someone and am stubbornly holding on to my position, I come back to the cross to be reminded again of how God works when we are willing to die to ourselves. When my love for the church grows weak or when I am frustrated with her failures and imperfections, I come to the cross and see again that Christ gave himself up for her. When I am reaching out to someone and am finding it hard to love unconditionally, I come to the cross and see the kind of love I must have.

For thirty years I have been coming to the cross, and yet, its power is undiminished. Each time I come, I am affected as though it were the first time. I find this remarkable. It is amazing that something God did on such a hated tree so long ago has the ability to put *everything* in proper perspective. It is incredible how it speaks to us whatever condition we are in— comforting, challenging, convicting—giving us just what we need the most. No wonder Paul wrote: "For I resolved to know nothing while I was with you except Jesus Christ and him crucified" (1 Corinthians 2:2).

My young Christian friends, let me urge you to stay near the cross. Go again and again to passages that describe it. Pay close attention to every communion message that focuses on it. Read books that take you deeper into its meaning. *If you are ever thinking about leaving Jesus, go back to his cross and spend a day there. You owe it to him.*

Through the years hymn writers have penned powerful words that have captured the cross' meaning, but perhaps no one has done it better than Isaac Watts in "When I Survey the Wondrous Cross":

> When I survey the wondrous cross,
>   on which the prince of glory died,
> My richest gain I count but loss and
>   pour contempt on all my pride.
>
> Forbid it, Lord, that I should boast,
>   save in the death of Christ, my Lord.
> All the vain things that charm me most;
>   I sacrifice them to his blood.
>
> See, from his head, his hands, his feet,
>   sorrow and love flow mingled down;
> Did e'er such love and sorrow meet,
>   or thorns compose so rich a crown?
>
> Were the whole realm of nature mine,
>   that were a present far too small;
> Love so amazing, so divine, demands my soul,
>   my life, my all.

Truly, we have no ground for boasting, save in what Christ did on the cross. Surely such amazing love always calls us to give him everything we have and everything we are.

24

Heaven Bound

And now finally,

During Jesus' ministry, he sent his disciples out to teach and to do what he had been doing with them. They cast out demons and did mighty things in his name. They came back absolutely ecstatic about the results. But then Jesus said something very interesting to them: "Do not rejoice that the spirits submit to you," he said, "but rejoice that your names are written in heaven" (Luke 10:20).

Later, the writer of Hebrews used the same language when he described those of us who are in the church as the ones "whose names are written in heaven" (Hebrews 12:23). What a great thought! When you signed on to follow Jesus, your name was written in heaven. The book of Revelation expresses the same idea by saying that the names of disciples have been written in the Lamb's book of life (Revelation 21:27). By the grace of God, your sins have been forgiven and your name has been written in heaven. Hold tightly to that fact. Keep it at the center of your thoughts. On those days when things don't go well, you can say, "This didn't work out, and that was a big problem. I don't have this figured out yet, *but* my name is written in heaven!" Remembering that your journey with Jesus will end up right in the middle of heaven has a way of changing your perspective on every tough situation you face.

A lot of things in this world don't live up to expectations. I remember a family vacation we took when I was a child. My dad and mom had saved in order to take me to what was supposed to be a great resort, a golfer's delight. We dreamed and planned for months. On arrival, our dreams were dashed. The place was a dump. The hotel rooms were dirty. Our modest local golf club looked like Augusta National compared to this course. The fairways were as hard as rock, and the greens were the worst we had ever seen. We played nine holes and asked for our money back. Heaven will not be like that. Heaven will far exceed even our wildest expectations:

> *"No eye has seen,*
> *no ear has heard,*
> *no mind has conceived*
> *what God has prepared for those who love him"*
> *(1 Corinthians 2:9).*

This passage that Paul quotes was originally written to describe the coming kingdom of which we are now a part. However, it well applies to heaven. We simply cannot conceive of all the glories and wonders that are in store for us. We cannot imagine the greatness of the relationships with God and with our brothers and sisters that we will enjoy forever. God has prepared something for us there that you and I cannot afford to miss.

Occasionally I talk with people who have fears that heaven will be boring. That is one thing I am confident that it will not be. Just look around at what God has created. Thumb through several copies of *National Geographic*. Look at the endless variety of plant and animal and human life. Look at the spectacular scenes: the Grand Canyon, Victoria Falls, the Swiss Alps, just to name a few of thousands. Look into the night sky and consider the awesomeness of the universe. Realize that what you see from the vantage point of planet Earth is a tiny introduction to the wonders of God.

We just do not have the ability to grasp all of what God is going to do with us and what he will show us. God's creativity knows no bounds, and in heaven his creativity will be bursting out all over the place. This I am sure of: No one there will ever complain of boredom. Boredom will be as absent in heaven as sorrow, pain and tears. Jesus said he came to give us life to the full (John 10:10). That full life has already started here in the kingdom of God on earth, but it will be taken to levels beyond our imagination in heaven. Whenever Jesus talked about heaven, he often used the image of a great banquet or a great feast. That was just another way of saying that heaven is going to be a blast. It will be the mother of all parties. Do you remember that party I told you about that you started in heaven? Well, one day you will be there, and you will see what a celebration really looks like.

There is an old criticism of Christians that says that they are so heavenly minded that they are of no earthly good. That was leveled at people who claimed to be Christians, but spent all their time dreaming of heaven and not working to solve the problems on earth. That was never God's idea. He has called us to be involved with every human problem and to bring to this world the only answers that will really make a difference. At the same time, we should continually be inspired by the thought of heaven. Peter had the goal of rousing the Christians when he wrote:

"Therefore, prepare your minds for action; be self-controlled; set your hope fully on the grace to be given you when Jesus Christ is revealed" (1 Peter 1:13).

Setting our minds on the amazing blessings at the end of the journey can be a powerful encouragement for us to work hard and give our best effort right now.

Is it worth it to sacrifice and suffer for the kingdom of God? Just consider heaven!

Is it worth it to say "no" to sin and to fight to live a life of purity and righteousness? Just consider heaven!

Is it worth it to stay in the race when it would seem so much easier to quit? Just consider heaven!

Is it worth it to give time and energy and tears to help others become Christians? Just consider heaven—not just for yourself, but for them!

The song says, "When we all get to heaven, what a day of rejoicing that will be!" On that day you can be sure no will be asking "Was it worth it?"

So my young Christian friends, stay on the narrow road. It leads to life. With the help of God and your brothers and sisters, fight the battles you need to fight. Deal with sin again and again. Make it your goal every day of your life to please God. Stay open to learning anything and everything he wants to teach you. Come back to the cross day after day after day. Share the good news of Jesus with as many people as you can. Do all you can to bring others to him. And when you get to heaven, let's all meet in the north corner of glory, where the party will never end.*

---

* We are indebted to our friend Jane Pattison Cicerchia for this idea. She has gone there ahead of us and inspired Robert Duncan to write the song, "The North Corner of Glory."

WHO ARE WE?

Discipleship Publications International (DPI) began publishing in 1993. We are a nonprofit Christian publisher affiliated with the International Churches of Christ, committed to publishing and distributing materials that honor God, lift up Jesus Christ and show how his message practically applies to all areas of life. We have a deep conviction that no one changes life like Jesus and that the implementation of his teaching will revolutionize any life, any marriage, any family and any singles household.

Since our beginning we have published more than 100 titles; plus we have produced a number of important, spiritual audio products. More than one million volumes have been printed, and our works have been translated into more than a dozen languages—international is not just a part of our name! Our books are shipped regularly to every inhabited continent.

To see a more detailed description of our works, find us on the World Wide Web at www.dpibooks.org. You can order books by calling 1-888-DPI-BOOK twenty-four hours a day.

We appreciate the hundreds of comments we have received from readers. We would love to hear from you. Here are other ways to get in touch:

Mail: DPI, 2 Sterling Road, Billerica, MA 01862-2595
E-mail: dpibooks@icoc.org

FIND US ON THE
WORLD WIDE WEB

www.dpibooks.org
1-888-DPI-BOOK